FAITH-BASED MENTORING

A Manual for Working
with Troubled and Delinquent Youth

Don Smarto

©2007 by Don Smarto

Published by Frontline Press
P.O. Box 764499
Dallas, TX 75376

Printed in the United States of America

ISBN 1-4243-2342-8

Library of Congress Catalog number: 2004108981
Printed in the United States of America

Unless otherwise indicated Scripture quotes are King James Version
of the bible. NIV are from the Holy Bible; New International
Version, Copyright 1978 by the New York International Bible
Society. TLB is the Living Bible Paraphrased, Copyright 1971 by
Tyndale House Publishers, Wheaton, Illinois.

Cover photos taken by Cecilia Bolar.
Photo models: Jason Bostic and Frank Ciola.

To Gloria Beyers,
my number one cheerleader!

Gloria was my mother-in-law. Among stand up comics, that is grist for the comedy mill, but those who really knew her saw a woman of faith, generous to a fault, with a genuine heart of gold.

I miss her greatly because she was my cheerleader. She was the first person to read one of my new books and the first person to spot a typo but she never failed to tell me how great it was.

When you get to my age, you would think that praise is no longer needed, but that is simply not true. Gloria was an encourager and that is what a mentor basically is. I always knew she was in my corner. She was someone I could count on. Even if she couldn't solve a problem, I knew she cared and was praying.

Don't misunderstand; she was not perfect. We could argue politics or theology for hours, and just as quickly laugh and share a meal. When the daily battle of life got me down, or the darts of the enemy stung, she was on the sidelines cheering "You can do it! Don't give up! Look to Jesus!"

I dedicate this book to her memory with my love and the words *Thanks, Mom!*

Also by Don Smarto

Justice and Mercy
Tyndale Publishers, 1986

Pursued
InterVarsity Press, 1992

Setting the Captives Free
Baker Books, 1994

Keeping Ex-Offenders Free
Baker Books, 1995
Revised: Frontline Press, 2001

Lost and Found
Frontline Press, 2003

Family Secrets
Frontline Press, 2004

To order additional copies of **Faith-Based Mentoring** or any of the
above titles, please contact:
Don Smarto
P.O. Box 764499
Dallas, TX 75376-4499
Fax: 972-572-8335
Phone: 972-572-8336
don@youthdirect.org

ACKNOWLEDGEMENT

As a writer, periods of inspiration have been sporadic. Most of the time, writing is just hard work. Truth be told, writers are fortunate to have support staff that can make sense out of first drafts.

Sue Ann Reynolds has been the recipient of my heavy breathing for some time. Please don't misunderstand. I talk into a dictation machine as I pace in circles getting my ideas out, and Sue patiently listens and transcribes the thoughts. By the fourth or fifth draft, I correct a hard copy with red ink and she formats the book. Only she knows how disjointed the material is. The cut and paste routine is never easy but she has never once complained.

We have worked together on five books and we have known each other for nearly seven years. I am proud to call Sue my friend. Many walk into and out of our lives with little impression, but not Sue. She started as a "temp", as my administrative assistant, in a work environment that was poison. She kept her dignity and her cool when most would have crumbled.

I thank God that we have worked together these years. Sue became the greatest treasure from a chaotic situation and reaffirmed for me the meaning of loyalty. If the book *Faith-Based Mentoring* seems logical and the thoughts progress naturally, thank Sue Ann Reynolds.

FAITH-BASED MENTORING

Table of Contents

INTRODUCTION

"Mentors inspire self trust."

Anonymous

INTRODUCTION

I felt very privileged in the spring of 2005 when I received a call from Governor Jeb Bush's office, the Governor of Florida, to participate in the announcement of a new faith-based mentor program with juvenile delinquents in the State of Florida. Subsequently, I had the opportunity to sit down with the professionals of the Florida Juvenile Justice system, including Kristy Bauer and John Sherman, and after stimulating dialogue, I was asked to write the training manual for their mentoring program.

For obvious reasons, state government must not favor one religious group and the manual had to be edited.

I have taken the core labor and research I put into creating that manual into this new book. I am pleased to make additions for a Christian faith-based approach. There are new chapters that assist mentors and mentees in finding churches and setting spiritual goals that will be useful to volunteers who come from churches.

As the leader of Youth Direct, an evangelistic program that has been in 160 juvenile facilities in 10 states, I know that evangelism must be coupled with discipleship. Many of our volunteers mentor youth.

Mentoring is more than simply the new "buzz word". It is about a relationship that an adult invests in a young person, which produces the real change necessary for them to become stable citizens.

Evangelist Dallas Anderson has said this, "In evangelism the goal is not to make converts but disciples, people who will not simply follow but will lead others to Christ."

It is important to say what I could not say in a secular manual, that as a mentor, prayer is essential. You must pray for the relationship. Pray that the Spirit will guide your words, helping you to speak and telling you when to not speak. And pray, by name, each day for your mentee.

Having worked in the juvenile justice system, I know that staff can sabotage the efforts of Christian volunteers. They can negate our message. They can distract by blaring communication radios. They can look disinterested during programs. They can even teach their own brand of secular humanism to the young people, which at the very least can confuse them.

That is why Christians must not only model to incarcerated youth but to the staff's needs as well. Sometimes their needs, although different, are just as great. They need Christ just as everyone does.

Dallas Anderson goes on to say, "Evangelism is a process, not just the harvest moment. We must take people from ignorance to full acceptance."

I have had the personal experience of mentoring over 12 young men. I maintain contact with many of them over the years.

Mentoring is not something that happens by chance. It is something that God has planned and in that sense "calls" you to touch a life and to change the world in one small place at one time. That is ultimately how we build the kingdom of God on earth: in a small place, one life at a time. God cares about relationships.

As a mentor, you play a crucial role as a bridge from the residential phase to a youth's return to home and their community.

Most of the juvenile justice systems that I have witnessed across America are committed to the rehabilitation of youthful offenders. That is the very basis of the juvenile justice system, which the U.S. Supreme Court affirmed after the Gault Decision in 1967. During the residential phase, whether they are in a minimum or high-risk facility, professionals are committed to the care and treatment of youth and ultimately have them engage in productive behaviors resulting in not returning to crime.

The professionals in Texas, Florida, California, Pennsylvania, Illinois and many of the other states I have visited believe that these youth can change.

These youth are not career criminals and will not become such when surrounded by caring, supportive people like yourself.

As a mentor you will have a relationship with the youth, depending on your state, both during the residential phase and after release. Even if your state does not allow both, the opportunities are meaningful. Many residential programs such as the ones I have visited in Texas and Florida use cognitive behavioral therapy, and it is compatible with the recommendations for mentoring you will find in this book.

Whether you represent a faith community or you are a concerned member of the community, I believe we are all in agreement that these young people can change and change for the better. I also believe that faith communities and government can partner together. The ultimate goal is for these young people to return to the communities as stable and productive citizens.

Volunteerism is a mighty force across America. The differences and diversity that each mentor brings strengthen and enrich us all.

This book has been arranged in small, easy to read chapters that you can use as a quick reference and as a manual as you progress in your mentoring relationship. They are meant to be practical, but always consult with those who are the program coordinators of the mentoring programs you are involved in. Never hesitate to ask staff any question.

There are so many single moms and hard-working parents that cannot do everything for their children. Teachers already have too much on their plate. That is why it is essential for mentors to be involved in the lives of troubled youth. In California alone there are 75,000 youth on a waiting list to have a mentor. We know that there are 14 million children under the age of 18, of which 1.5 million have a high need for a mentor.

Over the years research has shown that a stable mentor/mentee relationship will increase self-esteem, contribute toward educational success, and help a youth turn away from alcohol, drugs and gangs.

I believe you can summarize mentoring in three simple words: *someone who cares.* There is nothing more important for a young person than to know that someone really cares about them.

I was once speaking to a group of 10-year-olds confined in a large state facility. I told them a story from the Bible, and at the conclusion a young boy raised his arm and said, "That was a very good story, was it true?" I was startled. I had assumed he knew I was telling him the truth. People come to our churches and give their testimonies and we do not second-guess the truthfulness of what they are telling us. But youth do not automatically accept authority or believe in the truthfulness of adults. And that is because so many of these troubled children have been deceived.

When an absentee father tells a young boy or girl he is going to come for their birthday, and the child sits on the couch at noon, and at two, and at four, and at six p.m., and the sun sets but the father never shows up, they get to a place where they do not believe everything they hear because so many promises have been broken.

Mentoring reestablishes trust. It is based upon a relationship. I know that you take your mentoring relationship serious, and it may be the one factor that makes the difference between a youth that makes it and those that do not.

My expertise is working with juveniles, but I have found over the years that the principles are transferable with adults. In fact, many of the juveniles in the system go up to the age of 21 and young adults in adult jails start at 17. So one can see there is an overlap of the populations. Also, there are many in jail or prison in their late 20s who are still acting like an adolescent. They are not functioning at their chronological age. This is to say that most all of the principles you will find in this book are transferable and can be adapted to mentors who work with young adults coming out of jails and prisons.

Perhaps the sections on youth culture, their fascinations with technology, and being involved with juvenile gangs may not seem to fit, but all of the adults were once teenagers. And a great majority of them were in the juvenile justice system. I believe you will find the transference of ideas and concepts easy.

Here are some basic mentoring principles:

1. It is important to have parents who are willing to participate in a mentoring program, at least by attending meetings and being supportive of the young person meeting with their mentor.

2. Developing a strong, supportive network for mentors is crucial. There should be ongoing training and frequent contact with the mentors. Remember that a "bad" mentor relationship can harm a child and increase anger and mistrust toward authority.

3. The match is crucial. After properly screening the mentor, there should be shared interest for the relationship to initiate well. As an example, if the teenager loves basketball and the mentor hates sports, that may be a detriment. If the mentor is open to going to a basketball game and learning from the youth, then that can be overcome. Likewise, if a mentor loves classical music and forces the youth to attend a symphony, that can also be awkward. There can, of course, be an educational process as part of the relationship, but the compatibility of interest is important for a good match.

4. Some programs use PROCESS and others use RESULTS. As an example, the mentoring used by established programs like Big Brother/Big Sister, Teen Outreach, Here's Life Inner City, Match Point, Amechi, and Partners in Education use measurable goals like reduction in truancy, school attendance and better school grades. Research indicates that such relationships may not be as successful after five years as those that focus on the process, which is to say building trust and relationships.

5. It is good that those who coordinate the program have been mentors themselves so it is not purely theoretical.

6. Mentors and those who coordinate the community side of the program should be members of a local church and growing in their

own faith. A good question to ask a potential mentor is, "Do you have a mentor?"

7. There is a difference between a faith-centered and a faith-saturated approach of mentors. Faith-centered really means it is part of a person's core belief system, and it will naturally come out even when not talking about religion per se. A faith-saturated situation might be a person who is forcing the issue in trying to make every subject somehow relate to the Bible or to God. That can seem forced and be uncomfortable for the youth.

8. Not all boys have mothers, not all girls or boys in the criminal justice system have stable parents. Even if they do, a mentor can be a special friend. And they can have an impact that can last a person's entire life.

Tiger Woods is, without exception, one of the great athletes and golfers of our age. When his father Earl Woods died at the age of 74, Tiger said, "My Dad was my best friend and my greatest role model, and I will miss him deeply." Obviously the relationship went beyond father and son and coach and athlete. Mr. Woods said in his own book *Training a Tiger,* "I made it very, very clear that my purpose in raising Tiger was not to raise a golfer. I wanted to raise a good person." His father would not let the young man practice golf unless he had done his homework first. Tiger himself said, "He was instrumental in helping me develop the drive to achieve, but his role as well as my mother's was one of support and guidance, not interference." Tiger best summed up his relationship and the impact of his father when he said, "My father was my best friend, my mentor, and perhaps my greatest support system."

I was recently talking via email with a former high school classmate. When I brought up school, which had been 47 years previous, he said, "I don't like to think about it. It was hell on earth. I was lonely and had no close friends."

I was also lonely and shy, but I look upon my high school years with great fondness because a teacher became my mentor. I dedicated my book *Pursued* to my teacher Sig Swanson. Although he died many years ago, his voice still plays in my head and his encouragement still rings in my ears. That is the effect that a mentor can have. Although I was ages 14 through 17 when he influenced me, he actually influenced me well into my adult years and today. I think my former classmate would not look so dismal on his high school years if he had had a mentor who had been an encourager and got him through those difficult years.

Consider this statement from a teen named Joseph; "Being a teen is very hard at school. I have to be bad in order to be considered cool. I sometimes do things that aren't good. I talk back to my teachers and have been disrespectful to them. I do want to be good but it is just too hard."

The Bible tells us that we want to do good but often find ourselves doing what is bad. That is why we need God and godly mentors.

If you are already a mentor, I hope the practical advice in this book will be helpful. If you are thinking of becoming a mentor, let me encourage you to become involved and not only change a life but change a small part of the world.

If you are a professional considering starting a mentoring a program in your residential facility or in your community, start small, let it grow naturally because the impact of one caring adult on one youth can make a tremendous difference for the community and the kingdom of God.

What is a Mentor?

"The only people who will be really happy are those who
have sought and found how to serve."

Albert Schweitzer

WHAT IS A MENTOR?

Professionals know from research and years of documentation, and mentors know from experience that mentor relationships are very effective with at-risk and high-risk youth. Mentoring programs help youth succeed academically, create more positive relationships with families, reduce incidents of drug and alcohol use and lower the likelihood of criminal behavior.

Wisdom

For some, the word *mentoring* is synonymous with wisdom. The adult is a person who has lived sufficiently to learn from their mistakes, has positive values, cares about youth and can encourage and affirm a younger person.

A Coach

For others, a mentor is someone who coaches or guides. Anyone who has ever achieved any success in a sport knows that the coach was able to point out weaknesses and errors and provide alternative strategies for solving problems. Ultimately the greatest coaches are a friend, a source of wisdom and a teacher. They encouraged young people and were a role model.

In this manual we are defining mentoring as a one-on-one relationship between an adult and a youth, usually under the jurisdiction of a juvenile justice system.

Worthy Goals

One important goal is for the mentor to help the young person achieve worthy goals. These will be mutually determined based on the abilities, potential, and motivation of the youth.

It is a benefit that you, as a mentor, are a neutral, non-related party. Sometimes young people in the system have had problems with authority. Police, probation officers, social workers, teachers, and even parents cannot always reach them where a mentor can.

Role Model

Above all, you are a positive role model. If you remember the film character Yoda in **Star Wars,** he was an older, wiser character who would guide the more impetuous Luke Skywalker. The animated Disney character Jiminy Cricket would try to guide the marionette-become-boy Pinocchio (who had been influenced by anti-social peers toward an excursion), to the consequences of Pleasure Island, a place of bad deeds.

Encouragement

Several recent films demonstrate the impact an adult mentor can have on a youth. A teacher encourages a teen to develop scientific skills in the film **October Sky.** Based on the book *Rocket Boys,* the youth grows up to play a significant role at NASA.

A teacher and a father affirm a young boy to pursue his passion for dance in **Billy Elliot** and he becomes, as an adult, a featured ballet dancer.

In **Saint Ralph,** A priest affirms a teen as he practices and pursues his dream of marathon running. Without the mentor's patience, Ralph would not have achieved many of his goals.

In all three films, an adult mentor plays the pivotal role of encourager and builds the youth's self-esteem. Also in each film, there are characters who pour cold water on the youth's dreams and potential.

There have been cynics in every young person's life that have sent messages of defeat and the acceptance of the status quo and mediocrity. Many youth believe they are "not worthy" or "good enough" to accomplish worthy goals and pursue a good life and career.

That is where you, the mentor, can help change negative thinking to positive goals through your relationship with a youth.

APPLICATION TO MENTOR

As a mentor, you have the opportunity to participate in a relationship that will help change the course of a young life from poor decisions and destructive behavior to a productive life. You are following in the footsteps of many societies and civilizations that have seen the value of mentoring for nearly 3,000 years. Volunteers like you can make a difference. Your patience and trust will build a relationship where change is possible. You have accepted the responsibility of becoming a coach, an encourager, and a friend to a young person who really needs you.

Chapter 2

JUVENILE OFFENDER'S PROFILE

"I've never met a person, I don't care what his condition,
in which I could not see possibilitics.
I don't care how much a man may consider himself a
failure, I believe in him for he can change the thing that is
wrong in his life any time he is prepared
and ready to do it."

Charles Spurgeon

JUVENILE OFFENDER'S PROFILE

Introduction

While each state will have slightly different rules for commitment, the profile of the type of youth who go to detention and state facilities is generally the same.

In large states such as New York, Pennsylvania, Florida, Texas and California, over 100,000 youth are referred annually to the juvenile court and probation department.

Police who specialize in working with juvenile offenders have some discretion at the street level. When a minor's violations are small, they can simply talk to parents or warn the minor. When the behavior is law violative, a complaint can be forwarded to a probation department.

There are **status offenders** that commit crimes that are only crimes for juveniles. Examples would be curfew violation, truancy, and use of alcohol and cigarettes. We call these status offenses because these behaviors for adults are not considered illegal. Status offenses are put in place to protect minors from more serious behaviors.

When a minor commits a crime that an adult can be arrested or go to jail or prison for, then they come within the jurisdiction of the juvenile court.

The great majority of offenses are resolved through putting youth on probation, bringing in resources such as counseling and social service agencies that may direct them toward a private drug program or even foster care.

In every state across America few of the youth who go into the juvenile court system actually go to a state facility. If this were not the case, there would be a need of many more buildings, staff and an incredibly large budget just to accommodate them.

Whenever possible, the juvenile court attempts to keep youth in their home or community with institutionalization only a last resort.

Technically, youth are not criminals and have no convictions. We refer to this as adjudication. When they are found "guilty", they become a delinquent and usually require some form of supervision. In the state of Texas, as example, only three percent of 100,000 youth that are referred to probation and juvenile court actually are sent to a facility. This is usually because they are violent or have not responded to other types of treatment.

In every state where the behavior is very serious, such as murder, there is always the mechanism of trial as an adult with a determinant sentence that may be as high as 40 years. Usually a youth is committed as young as 10, but once within the juvenile justice system can stay until the age of 21 or until they have responded positively to programming.

The following is a typical profile of juvenile offenders in America:

- **90 % are boys.**
- **10% are girls.**
- **The average age of a committed youth is 16-years-old.**
- **85% are functioning at a 5th grade level. (This means they are five years behind their peers in school, especially in the areas of reading and math.)**
- **40% are identified as needing special education services.**
- **81% have an IQ below the score of 100.**
- **39% have a high need for drug treatment. ("High need" is defined as the primary need; however, over 90% of the youth have used or abused an illegal substance.)**
- **36% have severe mental health problems. ("Severe" refers to a psychiatric diagnosis such as bi-polar; however, over 85% have a mental health problem in the areas of compulsion, depression, aggression and hostility.)**

- 76% have parents who were never married, are divorced or separated.

- 35% have a documented history of being abused or neglected. ("Documented" is the key word here. Emotional abuse and neglect often run over 90% of incarcerated juveniles.)

- 62% come from low-income homes. (The majority of youth in the system come from poverty and those from certain urban areas, below the poverty line.)

- 74% come from chaotic environments. (There are many ways to define "chaotic", but nearly all juveniles in the system come from dysfunctional families and often witness crimes including assault and battery and even murder.)

- 54% have families with histories of criminal behavior. (In many states, incarcerated children have at least one parent that is in jail or prison and have at least one family member in the criminal justice system. Those who have a parent in prison stand a seven times greater chance of being adjudicated a delinquent.)

- 49% have had two or more felony offenses in the past.

- 33% have committed violent offenses.

- These demographic statistics vary from state to state, but the breakdown of race in Texas is as follows:
    o 43% Hispanic
    o 33% African-America
    o 23% Anglo

- 35% admitted they were gang members. (The word "admitted" is the key word. It is estimated that over 80% of youth coming from urban areas are actively involved with a gang.)

This profile should not be interpreted as meaning those who come from poverty or a single parent home are likely to engage in criminal behavior. Without question, generations of poverty, welfare and criminal histories in families are major contributors to delinquency.

APPLICATION FOR MENTOR

If mentors have come from a very different background, socially and culturally, they must be sensitive to the issues that are apparent in these profiles.

Young people do not chose where they are born or the families they come from. In many ways, we must see them as **victims** in order to truly understand why criminal influence, drug abuse and gang activity became a part of their life.

Often they come from families with little or no education and therefore, no values for education.

If the youth becomes involved in the mentor's church, an accountability team, which would include a tutor to help them with reading and math, is very important for their long-term success.

Also, there are social skills, often called "people skills" that are necessary for success in our society. Appropriate eye contact, kindness and gratitude are all important in the job world and to function well in community.

Finally, this profile is not necessarily an obstacle to be overcome, since it is part of the history of the juvenile, but to give insight and understanding to the mentor. They include indications of emotional baggage or other areas where counseling and empathy are most needed.

Chapter 3

The Goals of the
Juvenile Justice System

"Never confuse a single defeat with a final defeat."

F. Scott Fitzgerald

THE GOALS OF THE JUVENILE JUSTICE SYSTEM

There are many mentoring programs in states such as Florida, Texas, California and elsewhere. Whether you are working with an existing mentoring program or you are a professional hoping to begin one in your institution or state, here are some of the overall goals that will contribute to a substantial reduction of juvenile crime.

Goals of a mentoring program in a juvenile justice program:

1. Upon release from the residential phase, to strengthen parental and family relationships with the youth.

2. To assist the youth in completing a high school education through attendance, good study habits, good grades, and respect for teachers and administrators.

3. Having mentors and others help as tutors to accomplish educational goals.

4. Having mentors assist with helping youth with practical social skills and life skills.

5. Recruiting mentors who will help develop a strong work ethic in youth, assist with the job application and obtaining of a job, and give guidance with money management.

6. Youth who totally abstain from the use of illegal drugs and alcohol.

In addition to the major goals, there are several important **supplemental goals:**

1. The development of the youth's spiritual life through attendance and participation in a faith community.

2.   The youth's desire to participate in continuing education at a community college, a trade school, or four year college.

3.   As a youth moves into adulthood, it is hoped the mentoring relationship will contribute toward the youth becoming a responsible spouse and a good parent.

APPLICATION TO MENTOR

There are many goals that contribute to the overall goal of a substantial reduction in youth crime. The ultimate value for the citizens of any state is a safer community by having at-risk youth become stable citizens with no future violations of the law. As a mentor, your relationship is a major factor toward achieving these goals.

Chapter 4

How is Success Measured?

"The measure of a man is not the number of his servants, but the number of people whom he serves."

Paul Moody

HOW IS SUCCESS MEASURED?

A mentor will certainly want to know how the relationship with their youth is perceived as successful. On a personal level, feelings and emotions are fine, but they cannot be analyzed or measured as empirical data.

Empirical Evidence

It is obviously essential that you as a mentor realize that you are having a positive effect on a young person's life. But there are reasonable, empirical, and observable behaviors that can be measured and that data will be collected so programs can be replicated in other parts of the state or country.

Recidivism

The most important measurement for this type program will be recidivism. That is a word that simply means a return to crime. If the youth you are working with commits no criminal activities, that is the desired and ultimate goal. Even not having police contacts (questioned about crimes) is preferred.

School

The job of a youth related to their age is full time attendance in school. No delinquency or skipping classes, finishing school work such as reports, projects, and getting acceptable grades are all a good indication of success.

Service

In addition, involvement in community or church activities and work that contributes toward community service are good indications of maturity and growth.

Attitude

Another important area is a change in attitudes. Going from beliefs that affirm antisocial values and behavior to conforming to law-abiding behavior and becoming a good citizen. A good citizen, even for a youth, has to do with basically respecting the rights and property of other people. We often refer to that as the "Golden Rule," but it is certainly one of the indications of a successful transition back into the community. It starts with a good attitude.

Anger Management

Since many youth who have been in the juvenile justice system have had a problem with anger, how they diffuse anger and deal with it appropriately is another indication of growth. Youth who previously had temper tantrums and threw objects, hit or kicked walls, and now refrain from physical expressions of anger, likewise, show progress.

Peers

As a mentor, you should watch closely that the youth abstains from gang activity, situations that can lead to drug use or alcohol consumption such as unsupervised parties, and to abstain from associations with peers that have antisocial values and exhibit antisocial behaviors. Keeping good company spells success for youth.

Family Relationships

Improvement in family relationships is very important. They must be reasonable. As an example, a parent who does not like bleached or long hair is only focusing on something superficial. Better listening skills on the part of both the parents and the youth, acceptance of family responsibilities such as picking up clothes, learning to wash dishes, load the dishwasher, wash clothes and even cook are all signs of responsibility within the family unit. All of these are observable and can be measured.

APPLICATION TO MENTOR

It is important for the mentor to complete reports in a timely fashion because they will indicate the areas that are observable growth to the mentor, handling anger, changes in thinking and attitudes and improvement in family communication and relationships.

The growth in the mentor/mentee relationship is also important as that can be observed as empirical data. The youth you work with is human and not a clone nor a robot. Some of the changes may be slow, yet progressive.

Continue to affirm and encourage and remember that ultimately it must be a youth's voluntary decision to make the changes discussed in this section.

Chapter 5

Mentoring: A Short History

"The greatest among men is always ready to serve and yet is unconscious of the service."

H. Dlavatsky

MENTORING: A SHORT HISTORY

Mentoring, the activity of an older, wiser adult helping a younger person, often a teenager, has been utilized throughout civilized history. The ancient Greeks, who were both philosophers and teachers, would have a small group of young men that they would tutor and, in the case of the philosopher Socrates, ask a series of questions that would lead to more questions and explore topics together.

It is known that Socrates was the teacher of Plato, and Plato was the teacher of Aristotle, and Aristotle was the teacher of Alexander the Great. Beyond philosophy, each was mentoring the younger person in ways to approach life, how to be analytical, and especially, how to grow in character. Being a good example was a value of the Ancient Greeks.

Because women were relegated as second-class citizens for many centuries, they were not a part of the formal mentoring program although older women helped younger women, especially with family duties, social responsibilities and parenting.

Jesus had a group of 12 disciples that he chose. He was their teacher and mentor and they, mentees. These were basically young men who traveled with him for a period of three years. While the New Testament of the Christian Bible does not use the word *mentoring*, it is clear that most of his teaching was by example, stories were often called parables, and a series of questions for the disciples, was unquestioningly mentoring. After the resurrection of Jesus, most of these men were ready to take roles of leadership based upon the Master's mentoring and forming of their character.

This tradition then carries forth in the early church. We see that tradition in the case of Timothy. In the New Testament Paul, a major figure, had three younger men who he mentors: John Mark, Timothy and Titus. In the case of Timothy, who comes from a good family, we hear about the mother and grandmother but there is no discussion about Timothy's father. He is either absent or perhaps not as good a role model as his mother and grandmother. We know that young Timothy felt that others were looking down on him because he was young and he was very timid. Paul encouraged him, brought him on trips and wrote letters to him, which gave good council and encouragement. He specifically told Timothy not to think little of himself because he was young and that he should live above reproach.

A young Greek youth named Titus had developed slowly and was mentored by Paul and some of Paul's friends. He also gave Titus good advice, such as avoiding arguments that would divide people, being a good example to others, practicing self-control and relating to different age groups.

In the case of John Mark there seems to be a falling out between him and Paul. We assume that as an intelligent and strong personality, Paul may have been impatient with John Mark. On a missionary trip he abruptly leaves and returns to another city. But later we see a reunion between Paul and John Mark, which tells us several things. Paul had learned to be more patient and another named Barnabas (which means "encourager") came along and became a mentor to John Mark. In this last example we see that both the mentor and the mentee can learn from their mistakes and can grow together.

In ancient Greek society, mentoring was encouraged and seen as a very valuable process and relationship. Odysseus was a man who went to war and had his only son Telemachus put in the care of a mentor who was an older and wiser man.

In ancient Greece, mentors were not only teachers but also friends of the youth and guiding them in basic good values. It is known that Roman generals and officers had mentors who would guide them in military strategy. In Medieval times there was a group called the Guild Masters. This group of craftsmen would teach, and sometimes share. Apprentices not only learned their craft, but they also learned social skills and even spiritual values from the older person.

At the time of the Renaissance in Western Europe, mentoring was closely related to students of adult artists, musicians, and writers. It is known that famous artists like Rembrandt, Titian and Raphael had a "school" which really was a group of younger men who were taught basic skills, refined them under the master's eye, and eventually painted in a style close to the master.

In Colonial America we see the continuation of this adult-youth relationship in the master craftsman/apprentice relationship. There were skilled adult craftsmen who had young men (apprentices) who would learn the art of shaping fine and precious metal, working printing presses, and many other trades and crafts, but also by agreement with the youth's family, cultivate manners, social skills, and character.

With the formation of the Boy Scouts and the Girl Scouts of America, clearly the most important part of the Scout Leader's role was that of mentoring. They were simultaneously a coach, an advisor, as well as someone who taught camping skills.

In the American Congress, ushers, pages, and young staff members watch the operation of a congressman or a U. S. senator's office and at the same time have access to a knowledgeable, political leader. Many future congressmen and senators often started as young staffers in their own state, in a congressmen's office or a governor's office. Many fine attorneys and even judges today started their career right after law school by being a clerk, either for a Supreme Court Justice or a Federal Judge. The clerk had many responsibilities in the area of research and even writing, but always had the opportunity to ask questions and receive constructive criticism so that they were guided as they formed their legal skills. Clerks and the judges they worked under may not have used the term *mentoring*, but clearly the mentoring style and philosophy was a part of the relationship and continues today to be a part of that role.

There have been formal mentoring programs in America since 1900. Today there are well over 2,000 active mentoring programs in America, most formed during the last twenty years. You will probably recognize the name Big Brothers and Sisters as an example but there are many others, some smaller, that help on several levels. There are military mentors and corporate mentors, executives who help younger, middle-management adults.

You are involved in one of the most dynamic mentoring programs. You are not only helping a young person but a young person who has perhaps had "two strikes out." By that, we mean they have made very poor decisions that have resulted in crimes that have brought them into the juvenile justice system and have resulted in residential placement either at a minimum, medium, or high security institution. Most of the youth in this type program have failed relationships with adults.

These youth, boys and girls, need the guidance of a stable adult figure like you. And they need this guidance more than most youth in America because often the youth who are incarcerated are lacking a father. We know that with boys in particular, the loss of a father, either emotionally or physically absent, can lead to feelings of abandonment or desertion. And certainly many young men have turned to anti-social gang leaders and even drug dealers as substitute father figures.

That is why the mentoring programs with the juvenile justice system are so important for these young men and women. They can change.

How do we know mentoring works? Think for a moment about your own youth. Some form of pushing limits and boundaries, called rebellion, is common for every teenager. But as an adult, any success that you have had in life, in career or marriage was because you had healthy relationships with caring adults.

For some of you it was a teacher, a parent, a coach, or a youth worker. Many adults who are successful today have had as a youth, an adult mentor who encouraged them, helped them with life skills and social skills. There have been many studies that show that adult mentors working with youth see positive behavioral changes.

The Big Brother/Big Sister program did an impact study in 1995. It showed that a youth involved with an adult mentor improved the youth's grades by 59%, and there was a 73% improvement in clear, positive goals of the youth.

A 1991 Ford Foundation Report on the Quantum Opportunity Program showed a reduction in truancy by 53%, reduction in the use of illegal drugs by 46%, and a reduction in skipping classes by 37%.

Faith-based mentoring has shown very positive results. The Kinship Program of Greater Minneapolis in a 1988 report showed youth having increased respect for authority, taking on more responsibility, acquiring positive social skills and more optimism.

- 61% improvement in responsibility.
- 61% improvement in respect.
- 70% improvement in social skills.
- 74% improvement in optimism.
- 72% increase in parent's optimism for their own child.

There are 65,000 adult prisoners in Florida; 152,000 in Texas; 168,000 in California; 42,900 in Pennsylvania; 65,000 in New York and 44,000 in Illinois, as examples. Where do they come from?

When you look at the thousands that are in youth facilities, we know that some will enter the adult system unless there is intervention. There are also hundreds of thousands referred to the juvenile justice system who need to be reached with mentoring programs.

Chapter 6

Mentor/Volunteer Benefits

"Fulfillment in life comes not by the love of power
but by the power of love."

Anonymous

MENTOR/VOLUNTEER BENEFITS

Volunteerism in America is a dynamic force. Millions of volunteers help non-profits, charitable organizations, and churches as they serve those less fortunate in the community: the poor, homeless, elderly and troubled youth.

By stepping up to the plate as a mentor, you have shown a great servant's heart. This means you are willing to give your time to someone who is not related to you and, at least immediately, may not show total appreciation for the time you invest in the relationship.

Thousands of volunteers have reported tremendous benefits from giving to others. It is a word sadly ignored in some circles; it is called *sacrifice.*

Health

There is actually a physical benefit. People who serve their communities, give back to others and mentor troubled youth, often feel healthier. They are at peace, anxiety is reduced and they have less physical symptoms including high blood pressure.

Blessing

Churches using the **Bible** use the word *blessing.* The word *blessing* is translated as bringing happiness. For many adults, the knowledge that they are making the world better than they found it is a very comforting one. They realize that even after they leave this world, they have invested in a life that is continuing to grow correctly and produce good families and children in the future. This is the concept of continuity; that we can give back to the community as people have given back to us. That is a very satisfying emotion for many.

Often proved empirically, mentors can take comfort in knowing that by changing even one life, they have made their own community a safer place to live for their own children and grandchildren.

Strengthening the Family

Many mentors acknowledge that one of America's weaknesses is the dissolution of the family unit. An aspect of the mentoring relationship is to strengthen family communication and family ties. This also brings tremendous satisfaction to a mentor knowing they have helped reestablish the authority of the parent and helped facilitate and strengthen the parent-child relationship.

Monetary

For those who itemize tax deductions, mentors and volunteers can often deduct their mileage and some basic costs of meals, entertainment, and telephone bills. But by and large, most people do not volunteer to be a mentor for the economic benefits, although they are entitled to them.

Longevity

The greatest benefit is in knowing you have contributed to a changed life. Some people have mentored for many years and have seen the youth of 15 grow into a 29-year-old adult with children that has become a good spouse and a good parent.

That is a tremendous blessing for a mentor to realize. Also, as mentor relationships grow, they sometimes last for many years. There are many stories of mentor relationships that have continued for 10 years and longer. And often the youth has truly become a friend to the mentor.

Legacy

As we get older we think about legacy. Legacy means what we have left behind. Have we created in any sense a better world than what we found? And mentoring offers one of the finest legacies to realize that you are helping future generations through the life that you have touched. There are other benefits, although they may seem intangible, such as making new friends, developing new skills, and even what the mentoring relationship does for our own personal growth.

Some of the best benefits from mentoring are always personal. They transcend a free parking space or a free lunch. It is the knowledge that our sacrifice has helped touch a young life and set them on a positive course.

APPLICATION TO MENTOR

As you recall your own childhood and your teen years you will think of caring adults that mentored you. Your participation in this program is your way of passing on what you yourself received. There is no pin or award certificate that can come close to the sense of satisfaction in knowing that you have made a difference in a young life. As we get older we think about legacy. Legacy is about what we leave behind. We ask, have we created a better world than we have found? Mentoring offers one of the finest legacies to realize that you are helping future generations through a life you have touched. There are many tangible benefits, such as developing new skills, our personal growth and making new friends, but perhaps the greatest personal benefit is knowing that the youth you work with will probably remember you the rest of their life and may even repay your kindness by becoming a mentor themselves some day.

Chapter 7

Responsibility to Program Coordinator

"Love is a decision to serve someone."

Donald Whitney

RESPONSIBILITY TO PROGRAM COORDINATOR

Effective mentoring programs have a program coordinator. Some work within an institution, some within the district or county, but these are important point people that volunteers are accountable to. Not all programs currently in operation have program coordinators, but this is a suggested template.

Training

The program coordinator will be responsible for recruiting volunteers like yourself and for providing training. There will also be opportunities for ongoing training that will be sent to you via mail and email. The program coordinator is available for questions or the expression of any concerns.

One of your responsibilities is to thoroughly fill out monthly progress reports that will be given to the program coordinator. They will be pleased to assist you should there be any questions regarding filling out the form.

Team

As part of a team, the program coordinator, the chaplain, the aftercare coordinator, treatment coordinator and probation officer are there to support and assist you. There will be a schedule of regular meetings, often monthly, to encourage and to facilitate group discussion with other mentors to share youth strategies.

As a voluntary program, not only the youth but the family is required to participate and the program coordinator will also communicate with the family as well as yourself.

During your visit to a residential facility the program coordinator will work with the residential staff to coordinate activities with the family and with yourself.

APPLICATION TO MENTOR

The program coordinator is your team leader and is there to assist and support you should you have any questions or concerns. As a mentor, you are not alone and will have the support of seasoned professionals.

Chapter 8

Mentor's Frequently Asked Questions

"Love in the heart wasn't put there to stay:

love isn't love 'til you give it away."

Oscar Hammerstein II

MENTOR'S FREQUENTLY ASKED QUESTIONS

Like anything new, mentors will feel more secure in some areas than others. Here are questions commonly asked by mentors:

1. **What if the youth won't talk to me?**

    Answer: You will find that by being patient and taking time, the youth will eventually talk as trust develops.

2. **What if the youth does not show up for a meeting?**

    Answer: This will obviously not happen in the residential phase but may happen in the post-residential phase. The expectations and guidelines must be clear from the very beginning and while one missed appointment can be overlooked, there have to be set consequences for future violations since your time is important.

3. **What if the youth has asked if I have used drugs or alcohol?**

    Answer: Some adults may drink socially, but not every personal question has to be answered. If you made some mistakes when you were younger, you can share that as an object lesson. You may have learned from experimenting with drugs as a teenager and that can be valuable sharing but do not give excessive detail.

4. **What if the youth asks for money?**

    Answer: This is one of the rules that must to be established from the beginning. You may refer to Chapter 39. It is perfectly acceptable to say "no" to a request for money. There is a difference between giving someone three dollars for a magazine or paying for a fast food lunch and buying a Play Station 2 or Ipod. It is better for the youth not to have any expectations about money from their mentor.

5. **What if we don't relate?**

    Answer: There are several measures that will be used to match you with the youth usually based on gender, family background and interests. But you still remain two distinct and separate people. If nothing positive is happening after several months, contact your program coordinator and discuss the issue. Usually patience is the best rule. Some relationships develop more slowly than others.

6. **What if my youth's family doesn't speak English?**

   Answer: It would be fine to bring someone with you that can interpret, and at the same time, find a tutor that can help family members to understand and comprehend basic English. It is best not to use the youth as an interpreter because in the case of a disagreement it is conceivable that the youth is not interpreting the parents correctly.

7. **What if the family of the youth does not have a phone?**

   Answer: While this is rare, contact in that case would be by mail or in person.

8. **What happens if the youth doesn't have a family?**

   Answer: A mentoring relationship can be very effective even if the youth is in foster care or placement. Anyone who has guardianship of the youth, a grandparent, an uncle, or anyone willing to communicate with you for the benefit of the youth is acceptable.

9. **What if I think the youth is suicidal?**

   Answer: Refer to Chapter 34. When in doubt it is better to inform the program coordinator and other members of the team. Also allow the child to fully express their feelings.

10. **What if the youth tells me they have used illegal drugs?**

    Answer: Like any crime, while under the jurisdiction of a juvenile justice system in any state, you must inform youth that you are obligated to pass that information on to a parole officer. There are certain topics of conversation that cannot be held in confidence and it is better in the relationship to let them know that up front.

11. **Can I go to school as a parent substitute for a meeting?**

    Answer: You should always encourage the parent to attend any teacher meeting or conference. You can join them but you want to be careful not to replace them. Some family members may even want you to take on that role. Nothing prevents you from communicating with a teacher, but whenever possible support a healthy family and the parents.

12. What if the youth talks derogatory about his or her parents?

Answer: As a mentor, stay neutral. You can listen to them vent, but always have empathy for both sides. You never want to take sides with the youth against the parents or any authority figure. Long-term, that will be destructive. Just tell them that you have heard their complaints and objections but do not agree with a negative assessment of a parent.

13. Will I get any support as a mentor?

Answer: Yes, part of the team's role is to provide you with answers to questions, provide ongoing training, and be a support network to you the mentor. The relationship between you and the youth is not meant to take place in isolation. Both you and the youth have accountability to a larger team and maintaining communication with your team members will give you important and needed support.

14. Should I avoid touching the youth?

Answer: There are some forms of touching that common sense would tell us are appropriate; the light touch of a hand on a shoulder, a handshake, even a quick hug celebrating an important event like graduation. But generally speaking, it is important to avoid anything that will have a sexual connotation. While this would seem obvious to most people, there is no place in a mentor/mentee for a massage or a backrub, undressing openly together (even in a YMCA locker room) or explicit discussion about sexual development.

15. What if the youth asks me sexual questions?

Answer: There are safe and generic ways to answer every question. As a mentor you would never talk about the mechanics of sexuality but you can talk about general principles of respect and even abstinence. Some mentors may have to address the issues of teenage pregnancy and rather than becoming alarmed or hysterical, you will want to help the youth with a solid plan that will not lead to an overreaction.

16. What if the youth is having gender identification issues?

Answer: The mentor should encourage a healthy self-image. If a child feels they are gay, the support team can assist with appropriate counseling. Always affirm the individual whatever their gender inclinations. It is better for the mentor to be a good listener, and refer this to other professionals available in the community.

17. Should I meet with the youth alone?

Answer: In the residential phase, of course you will be in the facility in view of the staff, but after release it is better to be in a safe and neutral place where there are witnesses. That can be a fast food restaurant or a local gym. Youth will tend to talk more if they are in a place where others cannot easily overhear. Until the relationship develops over many months, it is not wise to be alone with the youth in the event any allegations are made about misconduct.

18. How can I attend recreational activities if I cannot be alone with the youth?

Answer: You can couple with another mentor and go to a ballgame or a football game as a group. Providing that your program coordinator believes it is acceptable for certain youth to mix, the communal activities provide a safe haven as the relationship is developing.

19. Can the relationship continue after a year?

Answer: Yes, many strong mentor relationships have continued for many years. Mentors have watched a teenager go on to college, get married and have their own children. Some relationships have lasted a lifetime. Nothing prevents the mentor from continuing the relationship after the requirements of the program are over.

20. What if the parent or parents don't like me?

Answer: Your focus is on the youth and it is hoped parents will appreciate your efforts and you can work together. Sometimes a parent can be envious if a child looks up to you. Also, there could be a personality clash. For the sake of the relationship, keep respectful and never engage in any arguments or disagreements in front of the youth. It is not essential that you and the parents are best friends in order for the mentor/mentee relationship to grow and be strong.

21. Can a youth smoke a cigarette in my presence?

Answer: No, because as a minor, it is an illegal activity. Even if they are of legal age, you should set your own ground rule that may include your preference not to inhale second-hand smoke during your meetings.

22. Does honesty mean I can tell the youth anything?

Answer: No, you must always exercise discretion. There are parts of everyone's life for which there is some regret and even shame. In order to help the youth it is not necessary for a mentor to divulge every bad behavior or mistake from the past. Be selective. Use only those examples that serve as an object lesson. Do not try to impress the youth with how "bad" you were when you were younger.

23. Can I introduce the youth to my family?

Answer: Yes, that should happen as a natural process. While it is not a goal of the mentoring relationship to "adopt" the child, an overnight stay with your spouse in the home can happen with the parent's permission. Even a weekend camping trip with other members of your family can be good. You are encouraged to invite the youth's family whenever possible to some events. There may be some cultural differences but many times they are overcome by a caring and compassionate attitude.

24. Can I give the youth a birthday and Christmas present?

Answer: There are ways to acknowledge an event without an expensive gift. You can certainly send a card and take the youth out for a meal, but be careful not to be excessive or to give them a gift that the parents or single mom could not afford to give. That might have the effect of making the family feel bad. After many years in a mentoring relationship, helping them with a college education may be acceptable, as the relationship has grown.

25. Should I ever call the police?

Answer: If you feel the youth has broken the law, start by talking to his or her probation officer and/or program coordinator. They would be the best people to judge whether going to police authorities would be the wise and proper action. Making a rash judgment call can really harm the trust of your relationship, especially if you are wrong about the behavior.

26. Are there any expectations during the visitation in the residential placement?

Answer: Like all residential facilities in most every state in the juvenile justice system, use common sense. Here are some guidelines:

- Since you want to be a good role model and start the relationship off on the best footing, arrive on time and always dress appropriately. For example, an adult does not need to wear a backward or tilted baseball cap. Do not wear expensive jewelry, and generally speaking, leave valuables (purses, wallets, briefcases, and cell phones) in your vehicle.

- Conform to the expectations of the staff in the facility. Sign in, show a government issued ID, wear the identification badge given to you. And when meeting with the youth, always make sure that staff can observe you.

- Double check to make sure that nothing in your possession could be considered contraband. Even a small penknife attached to keys can be dangerous in a facility. There is no need for you to have any medication, vitamins, or even tictacs on your person.

- The rules of the institution must be observed at all times. Do not bring unauthorized visitors or guests with you.

- Never comment on the system or administration. All youth will complain about some members of staff and certainly the accommodations and the food. By feeding into their attitude you are only making the youth more disgruntled. Totally avoid any comments about the juvenile justice system, the courts, the police, or whether criminals are treated fairly or unfairly. Such conversations will be quoted by the youth and they may even twist your words. It is far better to keep off the subject entirely.

- If in doubt, ask. That is always the best rule. If you do not know if you can bring food for the youth or a new pair of shoes, simply ask the staff and follow the facility guidelines and those you received in training.

APPLICATION FOR MENTOR

Never be embarrassed by any question you may have. There is no such thing as an insignificant question and your program coordinator will be more than happy to address any question or concern. As you review the preceding questions you will realize that you are not the first person to wonder about some of the potential pitfalls. Do not let them worry or concern you. Not all situations will happen in every relationship. These questions and answers are a "what if" scenario but are not necessarily a predictor of something you may experience.

Chapter 9

Mentoring Guidelines

"A great manager has a knack for making ball players
think they are better than they think they are.
He lets you know he believes in you.
He makes you get more out of yourself."

Reggie Jackson

MENTORING GUIDELINES

It is important to adhere to several basic rules that will contribute to the consistency and integrity of the faith and community initiative, which we refer to in this manual as the *mentoring program.*

Several areas are extremely important, and we will elaborate on each of those here.

Confidentiality

It is essential to maintain the confidentiality of the youth you are working with and any details about their past or their family. Obviously in bringing a youth to your workplace or church you can mention their first name, and as the relationship develops, eventually use the full name, but initially during the residential phase you must maintain complete confidentiality and protect the young person's identity.

Physical or Sexual Abuse

If the youth informs you that an individual is abusing them physically or sexually, you must inform them that you are obligated to report it. You can call 1-800-96-ABUSE or contact the coordinator of the program.

It is not for you, the mentor, to make the final judgment on whether the allegations are true or not. In some cases you may see symptoms of a youth acting withdrawn, a sudden mood change or you may see a bruise that may be an indication of physical abuse.

Do not attempt to be a psychologist and remedy the situation yourself. Do not keep the information to yourself, but share it with your program coordinator.

Voluntary

This initiative is predicated on the child and his family choosing to be in the program. It can only work when it is voluntary. There should be no aspect of the mentoring relationship that is mandatory. If the youth is resistant or no longer wants to be in the mentoring program, you may have discussion with the youth, family members and your program coordinator, but at no time should the youth be manipulated or made promises in order to remain in the program. Their withdrawal is not a failure on your part.

One-On-One

Mentoring programs like this one work best when it is one-on-one. You are developing a trust relationship, which takes time. Bringing in a friend or spouse for a recreational trip, event or birthday party is acceptable. But the relationship is not a group effort to the youth but is an individual one.

Reasonable Goals

It is important to have clear objectives that are reasonable, realistic and measurable. If the bar is set too high, the youth will experience frustration. If the bar is set too low, there will be no growth.

Violation of Rules

There should be clear rules so the youth understands his or her boundaries and the consequences of a transgression. As an example, you may require no use of profanity (an occasional slip is something that can be overlooked). You may require the person to show up for an in-person visit on time and set consequences for frequently failing to come at an appointed time. These rules will help the youth understand that there are conditions and responsibilities on their side for the relationship to grow.

APPLICATION TO MENTOR

As a mentor, review these important guidelines frequently. These are in no way meant to limit you and the relationship with the youth but rather serve as a structure which will keep you alert in these important areas.

Chapter 10

Church and State Partnership

"Love is the forgetting of oneself in the
service of another."

Ainsley Barnwell

CHURCH AND STATE PARTNERSHIP

There is really no violation of church and state when there is a working relationship between a faith community and a treatment initiative in the juvenile system because that would be a voluntary program. The program attends to all of the needs of a child, not only physical and mental, but spiritual as well. Faith is known by thousands of people across America to be a very powerful and positive force.

The fine programs used in the residential phase of a department of juvenile justice in most states compliments a faith-based mentoring program. It is not faith, or treatment, it is not "either/or". A person who has faith in God can still recommend the use of a psychologist, medication or counseling by a professional or hospitalization when appropriate. So just as faith is compatible with medical doctors when needed, the mentoring program and a faith component is totally compatible with what the state does through caring administrators and professionals.

Sometimes people believe that separation of church and state means that there should be no partnerships between churches and government agencies. This is not true.

President Ronald Reagan said it well in a speech he delivered in 1984.

> *"We established no religion in this country, nor will we ever. We command no worship. We mandate no belief. But we poison our society when we remove its theological underpinnings. We court corruption when we leave it bereft of belief. All are free to believe or not believe: all are free to practice a faith or not. But those who believe must be free to speak of and act on their belief."*

America's founding fathers never envisioned a country without religious values. They strongly endorsed appropriate interaction between the church and government.

History of Partnership

The program that you are involved in as a mentor does not violate any federal constitutional guidelines. Faith communities have played a crucial role in the development of American society. From the early days of our country, churches have been at the forefront of social reform, helping delinquent youth, providing shelter, care, establishing hospitals and medical services for the poor, and refining America's educational system.

No State Environment

Our founding fathers had a deep commitment to their personal faith and encouraged the faith of American citizens. People are free to believe or not believe. By reacting to a state established religion, as was the case in England, they were careful to establish that the government or state cannot sponsor a particular religion.

This is where people sometimes are confused. Our constitution does not ban faith communities from working with government but rather encourages faith practices and sees the value to the community. That is why all the currency of America still bears the motto "In God We Trust". All faith communities bring great value to America and to our citizens. Whether you belong to a faith community or not, what government and church agree on is the ultimate goals for these youth.

Ultimate Goals

Both the faith community and government do not want these youth to return to crime, to shun gang activity and the use of illegal drugs, to complete their education and to someday become stable parents and spouses. No one can disagree with the goal of youth that have stronger family relationships, develop a good work ethic, find a meaningful job, and become taxpayers rather than tax 'takers'. We all want to see today's youth become stable adults who are also good American citizens. That is why this mentoring program is able to have a working partnership between church and state.

APPLICATION TO MENTOR

States like Texas and Florida have innovative faith and community based programs for delinquent youth. This faith and community based initiative is a partnership with government because our goals are the same. They both want the lives of youth to be transformed, for communities to be empowered and for citizens to live safely in communities with a reduction in youth crime. As a mentor, you are participating in a unique collaboration that partners government with faith and community groups. In the Old Testament the prophet Isaiah said, "Here I am, send me." You have responded as a servant. Your caring is going to make a great difference.

Chapter 11

Faith Boundaries

"The task of the modern educator is not to cut
down jungles, but to irrigate deserts."

C. S. Lewis

FAITH BOUNDARIES

An important theme of the mentoring relationship is mutual respect. As a mentor, it is important to respect the wishes and the freedom of choice that the youth has.

Take Time

The youth may express an interest in your church. It is fine to bring them to a religious service, but communication with parents is also vital. Always avoid rushing the process and stay with major themes rather than minor ones. In some churches, as an example, speaking in tongues is valued. Some denominations will argue over different types of baptism (infant, sprinkling, total immersion). But as the youth's awareness of his or her spiritual life develops, their belief system should evolve naturally. There should never be a rush to a sinner's prayer, an "altar call," a commitment to a specific church, to be baptized, or church membership.

In time, as a youth looks to you as a role model, they may see a benefit that your faith gives you, such as peace and joy, and they will ask leading questions wanting to know more. That is the appropriate time to answer such questions.

Be Supportive

The rush to join a particular church can even be seen as threatening to a parent. And if the church that is chosen is a different denomination or even a different religion than that of the parent, it needs to be approached sensitively.

Obviously, having the youth become part of a faith community can help their stability and their growth, but as said previously, it should never be rushed or pushed as an agenda.

Talk to your program coordinator and the chaplain if you have any questions about how to proceed regarding the spirituality of the youth you are mentoring.

Even unchurched youth may have faith beliefs. "Never underestimate the spirituality of a teen. If I expect that I will encounter God in them, I will get a lot further than if I see the devil in them just because that's how they're acting" (Greg Morris, Episcopal Youth Worker). Their spiritual journey is highly personal but needs guidance. God must not become just another authority figure to rebel against.

A long-term commitment to a church or faith community can be a major, positive contributing factor to the youth's stability. Whether attending a mosque, a synagogue, a cathedral or a Bible church, a youth can discover lasting moral guidelines and accountability that will help the youth both in the short term and for their adult life.

APPLICATION TO MENTOR

A teenager can unquestionably have a spiritual life, and the youth you work with can be guided by your personal faith and association with a faith community. It is best to answer spiritual questions when the youth asks them and to let any contacts with your church evolve from the youth witnessing the impact it has on your life. During the residential phase the chaplain can advise you as to any religious choices or major decisions the youth has made.

Chapter 12

Mentoring High-Risk Youth

"There is a destiny that makes us brothers,

none goes his own way:

all that we send into the lives of others

comes back into our own."

Edward Markham

MENTORING HIGH-RISK YOUTH

While there are many types of mentoring programs in the business community and in the military, the mentoring of high-risk youth, in particular youth in the jurisdiction of a juvenile justice system (currently in a moderate, medium, or high-security level facility), present particular challenges for the mentor.

Sub-Culture

It is important for the mentor to understand that this is not a mainstream young person signing up for Boy Scouts or Girl Scouts. The youth has a track record of criminal behavior. Understanding what is the background of the at-risk and high-risk youth will help the mentor's sensitivity and develop a strategy.

The program coordinator will give you, the mentor, as much background information as you will need in order to develop positive goals within the mentor/mentee relationship.

Following are some of the common behaviors most youth will have in their background:

1. **Truancy** – Many of the youth in the juvenile justice system have had problems in school that have resulted in truancy. As a mentor you can help them renew interest in basic subject matter and show them the relationship between education and a good job.

2. **Poor Grades** – Many of these youth have not experienced academic success. For different reasons, including poor nutrition or a lack of parental involvement in schoolwork, these young people have come to dislike basic subjects like math and English. As a mentor you may not have been proficient in these areas, but you are functioning at an educational level far above that of the youth. You are not only able to assist them in most school curricula where they are struggling, but in the larger community you may recruit tutors who are willing to volunteer their time to assist the youth.

3. **Reading Level** – Frequently youth in the juvenile justice system are reading far below the level of their chronological age. Many are reading at a third grade level. The ability to read is not only important in education, but also as they seek a job, understand and properly interpret a job application, fill it out correctly, and communicate in a clear manner. As a mentor, showing the relationship between reading, writing and functioning in society will help them as they form worthy goals.

4. **Drugs and Alcohol** – The majority of youth in this program have had some problems with abusing alcohol and drugs. Some have been in treatment programs. Others have merely experimented. But those who have been influenced by peers have come to believe that the use of these substances is *normal*. Sometimes a parent has had an addiction or a problem with drugs or alcohol and youth witnessed a poor role model in their own home. For a minor, abstinence is the correct message because smoking, using alcohol, and drugs are illegal for them. Never send the message that "a little pot" is good for stress. This would be counter-productive and could be taken by the youth as license. At the same time, preaching about the evils of drugs and alcohol is not going to immediately solve a problem. It is better to realistically talk about the consequences and give them alternative sources of happiness and joy that come from life without these substances. Be a good listener.

5. **Neglect/Abuse** – Some of these youth have experienced neglect or abuse and it is important to be sensitive to how they may view or even mistrust authority figures. As an example, a young girl who was a victim of incest will not have the same reaction to the phrase "God the Father" as a normal church-going youth might. They will relate the word *father* to their own experience. And their own experience may have been a father that abused or violated their trust.

Only talk about past neglect/abuse as it surfaces and do not force the subject. If it is a current problem, refer to the section in this manual of Mentoring Guidelines about *Physical or Sexual Abuse*.

APPLICATION TO MENTOR

The youth you work with have had problems with cognitive skills, which is to say their thinking abilities. They have made poor decisions and have been impeded in making goals because of a frequent desire for instant gratification. Understanding their actual reading level, their negative experiences in school, their use of drugs and alcohol and any neglect or abuse will help you to be sensitive to a special group, unlike mainstream teenagers.

Chapter 13

Adolescent Development

"We know that teens are going to move away
from their parents.
The question is, Where are they going to move to?"

Reverend Bryan Wilkerson

ADOLESCENT DEVELOPMENT

As an adult, if you think back to your own teenage years, you will easily remember that they were years of excitement mixed with confusion and even awkwardness.

Puberty

Coming of age, biologically referred to as puberty, takes on all the physical characteristics of an adult body with some remnants of a dependent, emotional child. While there is rapid physical growth, there is the struggle between dependence, needing the parents to provide shelter, food, clothes, and the striving for independence, which is normal and natural.

The teenager wants to become their own person and sometimes will accept values different from parents just to assert their individual boundaries. Some rebellion is natural during the teenage years, pushing limits and boundaries. The youth that you work with has specifically made poor decisions, and have been adjudicated for crimes that reflected antisocial behaviors. Whether within a sub group or as an individual, the treatment program in the residential phase of a juvenile justice program has been directed at helping them to make good decisions, appropriate thinking and develop appropriate values.

Let us consider some of the stages of adolescent growth:
1. **Physical**
2. **Social**
3. **Spiritual**

Physical

The physical or biological state of adolescence has been dramatically shifting younger in the last few years because of better nutrition. While the onset of puberty was generally accepted as age 13, with every generation the physiological maturity has come younger from generation to generation. The onset for puberty in girls is dropping to 12.1.

Some scientists think it is the effect of the environment and substances that have estrogen-related physiological effects. Others look to diet and better nutrition. Boys are reaching adult heights at a younger age as well, which may also reflect better diets.

One of the areas that brings both confusion and excitement for teens is sexuality. Our culture is more surrounded by sexual symbols whether the Victoria Secret window in the shopping mall to explicit ads and billboards revealing fashions. The knowledge and experimentation in areas such as oral sex were virtually unknown several generations ago. Internet pornography is seen by many teenagers.

An early adolescent, ages of 12 and 13, are far more concerned with fitting in socially and are obsessed with appearance, being awkward, overweight, and the number one producer of anxiety—acne.

In mid-adolescence, 14 and 15, they begin to deal with concepts such as justice, right and wrong, and patriotism versus nationalism.

In later adolescence, ages 16 and upward, learning how to drive becomes important as is the need to fit in with peers. Important issues such as dating, sexual experience, pregnancy, and contracting sexually transmitted diseases are also important at this age.

Teenagers compare themselves with peers. Some are athletic, and others are awkward. Some develop secondary sex characteristics very early and some very late. Their physical growth often determines much of their self-esteem. Because of hormonal changes there are also wide mood swings and extremes of emotions.

Social Development
There are many social adaptations that take place in the adolescent. As previously stated, they are developing an individual identity that is separate from the family. This sometimes causes parents to feel a loss of communication or a "pushing away" on the part of the child.

There are strong bonds made with peers of the same sex and eventually the opposite sex during these years. During late adolescence there is a development of unique skills, which can later lead to a job and career. It is at this point they explore adult roles.

Spiritual Development

Early adolescence is a searching for absolute values. This is a useful time to discuss the basics of faith and many young teens make a decision to pursue a particular faith.

In middle adolescence youth will struggle with the notion of sin or guilt: having a sense of right and wrong, trying to obey the conscience but pulled by peers and others who would influence them in antisocial behaviors. Guilt is also associated with sexuality activity from masturbation to sexual intercourse.

In late adolescence, as they become independent, their spiritual life takes on a new dimension. They are able to ask complicated questions. Considering a God who is taught as all-powerful and loving, they will sometimes question why God allowed Hitler to destroy so many lives, terrorism, criminal child predators, or why is there innocent suffering especially if they have a younger brother or sister with an illness like leukemia. Those who experience the early death of a parent through a disease such as cancer or a sudden heart attack may also begin to question the foundation of their faith.

APPLICATION TO MENTOR

It is important for a mentor to remember that adolescence is a time of rapid physical growth but also dramatic changes in their relationship to their family, a seeking of independence apart from the family, experimentation with sexual activity, drugs, and a need of acceptance by peers. While these are not subjects that need to be openly discussed with the youth, it is important information for a mentor to understand that some of the emotions and mood shifts are caused by hormonal changes and are natural and normal. By being patient, understanding and nonjudgmental, the mentor can help the adolescent as they emerge from this period of life that has dramatic physical growth as well as social and spiritual changes.

Chapter 14

Basic Needs of Youth

"Left to ourselves

we are at the mercy of our passions and fears."

William Barclay

BASIC NEEDS OF YOUTH

We are all aware of the basic needs of a human being. If you, as a mentor, think back to your own childhood, you knew that you wanted the attention and affirmation of your parents. You also wanted to achieve in school, either in sports, music, the arts, science or another discipline.

Growing up we had basic needs, such as food and shelter. Then the needs became more abstract and more goal-oriented as we became teenagers.

A psychologist named Abraham Maslow (1908-1970) had a theory that became very popular in the 1960s and can be utilized by mentors in this program.

Maslow created a pyramid in which he talked about the basic needs that every human being has. By putting them in a specific order, he made it easy to understand and we can apply his principles to how a troubled or difficult youth will react to needs not being met, especially when youth come from a dysfunctional family.

Physical

Maslow started at the base with *physical needs* as basic needs. This one is easy to understand. As adults we know that there are certain laws of nature we cannot cheat. You need sleep every day, and if you have ever tried to stay awake 48 or more hours, you know that you simply cannot function properly. This is equally true for youth and adults.

We know that we need exercise in order to have good muscle tone and a clear mind and a functioning heart.

Probably the most basic needs are for oxygen and water. A human being can go two to three weeks without food, but not very long without water. That need, which we call thirst, is going to override any other need an individual has. Thirst is simply the body crying for attention for what it needs to function. Instinctively the body knows that without water it will die.

Any adult mentor who is a parent and has raised a child knows that a baby is pretty much the center of its own world. It has a physical need and it will let you know, usually through crying. The baby wants to be fed, the baby is uncomfortable with a wet diaper and wants to be changed, the baby wants to be held. Certainly the need for nutrition is going to be overriding for an infant.

Mentors can easily assume that the basic physical needs of the youth are being met unless there is a reason to observe or suspect poor health or nutrition.

Security and Safety

The next level in this hierarchy is a level called *security and safety*. This principle is very relevant for mentors. Although we are not far up the scale, this is the area which if unmet, leads to anxiety and fear in people, in particular youth.

As an adult, you know you have a need for a good job, an adequate income for your cost of living, and you want to have both medical and life insurance and even savings for a retirement fund.

For youth, these security and safety needs are more fundamental. They are striving for independence, and in breaking away from parents are often insecure about whether they can support themselves. This is the internal struggle of the adolescent: needing the parent for basics like food and shelter, yet, at the same time wanting to push away and be independent. This is where the mentor can be helpful. You can assist the youth in that process of becoming an independent, young adult. It does not happen overnight. It is fraught with mistakes along the way.

An absent father or a single mom who is battling a drug addiction often affects a youth at this level. There is the fear that they themselves have become the parent (caretaker) of their parent. The mentor can help greatly to reduce anxiety and fear by showing that there is a caring adult in their life who will not let them suffer any loss of basic needs and community resources are available for their parents, too.

Belonging

The next level is called *belonging.* We are very aware that one of the most important needs for a youth is to have friends and to be accepted by their peers. The mentor plays an important role in this area by making them feel a part of the larger community. The need was met formerly by gang members or their own peer group, but in introducing them to a church and becoming part of a larger community that includes people of all ages, they begin to fit into the community. Many times when there is not a functioning family, the mentor can assist in putting together a church accountability team that is essentially a family substitute.

As a mentor you are not trying to substitute for a parent, of course, but many times the youth will see you in a parental role, especially when a parent is missing.

Without a sense of belonging, individuals grow up feeling lonely and alienated. In many of the 37 school shootings across America during the past decade, when looking at the psychological profile of the shooter, you will find a person who did not have meaningful connections to the community or to their family. This sense of being alone in the world can also lead to anger and rage.

Esteem

The next level that Maslow defined was *esteem.* We often talk about self-esteem, which means how we feel about ourselves. We are not confusing this with pride. Here again the mentor can play a fundamental role because as much as staff may try within a residential facility to treat youth as an individual, it is natural for the control mechanisms, especially in a high-risk environment, to force the youth to become part of a group. They have to form lines and walk together. They have rules that apply to all of them as a group. And although there are moments of individual attention and counseling, the mentor can really help in the transition phase between the facility and a return home by giving special attention to a youth.

In life the need for esteem is sometimes called "status." Adults seek an important job title or a good reputation in a community. Sometimes people enter a military career seeking glory. And often youth, influenced heavily by the music and video culture and looking at magazines geared toward teenagers, are looking for that most elusive bubble called "fame," sometimes coupled with "fortune".

Fame

Most adults know that fame is fleeting. There are very few people in our society that will ever become a Gold Medal Olympic Champion, the pitcher who wins the World Series through a no-hitter, a movie star or a rock star. While these goals are natural for that age, the mentor can really help to show all the steps that are involved.

Goals and Steps

Here is an example; a youth that says he wants to be a rock star often does not even play an instrument. The mentor can show how learning to play a musical instrument is a day-by-day process that involves a lot of practice. Once the steps are in place, a grandiose goal can become a realistic one. Perhaps the youth does not become a rock star, but becomes a musician playing in a high school band or in a church service. They may even go on to college and get a music degree and be a music teacher in an elementary or secondary school.

As mentors we have had goals when we were young that not very well grounded, but it was usually someone older in our life that helped us see all the logical steps involved in achieving something worthy.

It is always important that the goals you set with your mentee are clear and achievable. By having contact for at least a year, in person weekly, and during the week by phone or email, the relationship will grow.

Self-Esteem

Psychologists often comment that a lack of self-esteem is often at the root of many psychological problems. When someone feels inferior, out of the mainstream, or living on the fringe, it is easier for them to make bad decisions and even become involved with the criminal, anti-social element.

Faith Communities

Organized and historical religions meet many needs through structure and moral codes, especially spiritual goals.

The Ten Commandments of the Old Testament are directed at the family, not really the individual. Even "Thou shalt not kill" which seems to apply only to individuals has a bearing on the family, since 80% of all murders in America take place in a home by people who are related to each other.

This does not mean that as a mentor you are going to formally teach the Ten Commandments to the youth on day one, but you can slowly introduce them to this code, which has literally been used for centuries. You may often be surprised that youth who have been unchurched do not even know what they say or mean.

Many times you will be a sounding board. That means without making judgmental statements you will just listen to where the youth is and at appropriate times give feedback. In this way you will help to define their goals and separate those that are realistic from those that are unrealistic relating to the youth's basic needs.

You are also in a great position to bring other adults into the picture to help you coordinate resources. As an example, a youth who needs a job might be helped by another adult in how to fill out a job application or what would be appropriate to say during a job interview. There may be someone in your church that has a small company or a restaurant and can employ the young person. A mentor need not feel they have to meet every need of youth. By forming a team, both from the Department of Juvenile Justice and other adults from the workplace and from their church, they can point the youth in the direction of resources and have them take steps to help themselves.

Ultimately you want the youth to have a sense of empowerment, which means that they have the ability to make good choices without having to check with the mentor at every step. It will be very rewarding at the end of each month to find out that they may have made two poor decisions but eight really good ones.

APPLICATION TO MENTOR

As a mentor, you are in a position to use the two poor decisions as a learning experience while rewarding them for the good choices they made. Those choices may include resisting illegal drugs that were offered by a peer at school or doing chores at home even when not asked. Mentoring is a powerful tool to help a youth become a stable adult. In a juvenile justice program you are an essential bridge between the residential component and the return to home and community.

Maslow's definition of basic needs can be applied to your mentor relationship, especially understanding how youth develop anxiety and fears related to their needs for security and safety.

Chapter 15

Youth Worldview

"Treat people as if they were what they should be

and you help them become

what they are capable of becoming."

Johann von Goethe

YOUTH WORLDVIEW

Each of us has a worldview. That simply means that how each person sees the world is different from every other person. It is as if we see through a filter and that filter is the sum total of our experiences, where we were raised and by whom, and whether they saw the world optimistically or cynically.

Do not assume as a mentor you are seeing the same world the youth does. There are myriad cultural influences for today's youth that adults did not have to contend with when they were young.

Technology

Today's youth have always known a Walkman, an Ipod, a CD, or a cassette player that put music into their ears at all hours. The world of technology has made them very different from us. They live in a world of incredible visual and auditory stimulation but generally do not embrace reading. They live in a world of cable television with hundreds of TV channels, MTV, and all the good and bad aspects of computer technology.

Information

Youth are able to get information at incredibly fast speeds while at the same time chat rooms and instant messaging isolate them from real conversation and interaction with friends. Youth spend 8.5 hours a week chatting and e-mailing compared to 1.8 hours using the computer for schoolwork. We also know that movies, television and rap lyrics are often violent, and this violence has desensitized youth to the violence of every day life.

Family

While the word *family* has a good connotation for many of us, more youth are confused about the meaning of family today. Divorce is at a high rate. Many of the youth in America's institutions are being raised by a grandmother or a single mom. Natural fathers are often out of the picture. Marriage is being redefined. People are living together before making a commitment. And gay and lesbian parents (marriages) are becoming more common. Even in the world of dating, youth are expected to have a sexual experience or else they are "missing out" on what everyone else is engaged in, including sexual intercourse.

Emotional Wounds

If you are working with a youth that was neglected or abandoned, who had a parent with a drug or alcohol addiction, a young girl that was a victim of incest, or a youth who was physically or sexually abused, their worldview is going to be dark, ominous, and foreboding. They will not instantly trust authority figures and may confuse love with a sexual act. In these cases you must be incredibly patient and understanding. Even when a youth makes judgments or poorly words their criticism of your life, it is best to never take it personally. Mentoring works best when your acceptance is unconditional and nothing will cause you to reject the child, even a temper tantrum.

Worldview

It is of course good to have rules in the mentoring relationship that include no name-calling and no fits of anger, but occasionally a youth will slip up. For the mentor it is most important to understand that creating a relationship takes time because you literally come from different worlds. Yes, you live in the same physical world, but you do not see the world the same. That is what we mean by worldview.

Eventually as the relationship develops, they may come to view the church and God in as trusting a way as you do. They may also come to hold such values as patriotism and become citizens who participate in the electoral process and find areas of service within the community.

Perception

Do not let the differences in worldview become a chasm. There are bridges that link people from different backgrounds and different orientations. We call it love. Everyone needs encouragement and unconditional acceptance and the youth you work with is no different. While they may be tempted to see the glass half empty, as a mentor, you can keep encouraging them to see the glass half full by pointing out many of the good things life has to offer.

That is what is important about your role as a mentor. You are older. You have come to realize that the inevitable problems in life can simply be interpreted as challenges that can be overcome rather than personal attacks on an individual.

Redefinition

There is only one real way to understand worldview and that is to be a good listener. Studies have shown that adults interrupt a person who is speaking about once every 17 seconds to get in or to defend their view. By resisting and by listening for long periods of time you will come to see how they view the world, and when you do, you can begin to chart a course of action and help them refine their goals, and help them redefine the world in a more positive and optimistic manner, a positive worldview.

APPLICATION FOR MENTOR

A mentor is aided by understanding how the youth views the world. It is not the same world that you see as an adult. In addition, you are different people because of the experiences of the youth. Because many have struggled with difficult life experiences such as abuse, witnessing violence in the home, poverty and even discrimination, they may see the world as an unsure and unsteady place where not all adults are trustworthy. There is no better way to comprehend their worldview than to be a good listener. Understanding how the youth you work with sees the world will help you to move them from cynicism to trust and from a low self-esteem to hope.

Chapter 16

Mentor Activities Within Residential Facility

"Well being is attained little by little."

Zeno of Citium

MENTOR ACTIVITIES WITHIN RESIDENTIAL FACILITY

Be Yourself

There are several activities you can engage in that transcend simple conversation within the facility. Since the mentor/youth relationship is new, above all be yourself and never pretend to be something you are not. Do not wear an earring or get a tattoo just to look cool. Do not quote the lyrics of rap music that you ordinarily would not listen to. A youth will come to appreciate you for who you are and your life experience and they are the first ones to see through any pretense.

Photos

Many youth have photos and asking them to share some with you is a part of what is referred to as "phototherapy". Do not ask for any specific photo like family photos but see what they choose to share. Sometimes it may be a car that they worked on or painted. It may be a girlfriend. Or it may be a family member who died. Talking about their photos is a safe way for youth to begin to open up and talk about their own feelings. You may notice after one or two visits that they have selected photos of a particular person but have never shown you a photo of their father.

What They Talk Around

In psychology we sometimes realize that what people talk around or avoid may be the heart of a problem. You can make a simple observation "I noticed you have not shown me any photos of your father". It is an open-ended question and you may get an interesting and long response.

Most youth will be animated in the process of sharing their personal photos with you. As a response you may bring some photos with you, within reason, as a teenager. Early in the relationship, if you have small children or grandchildren, it is not best to share those photos or give personal family information. Likewise do not show them pictures of your house, cars or possessions. If you share photos, it might be even amusing for the youth to see your high school graduation picture. They may make fun of your loss of hair, but that is fine.

The important thing is getting off to a good start by being a good listener. If, in the first weeks and months, they develop an image of you as someone who lectures or preaches, it will be far more difficult to have the relationship grow in the post-residential phase.

Future Goals

Talking about goals is an important subject. Ask them to fantasize what they could be if there were no restrictions on time or money. Would they go to law school or medical school? If they settled for a minimum wage job at a fast food restaurant, try to find out what is limiting their goals. It may have been negative images they have gotten from other people and this is your first opportunity to begin to encourage them.

Everyone has had disappointments in life and the youth you work with are no exception. Because of their life experiences and family backgrounds, open-ended questions about what has disappointed them in life can be very revealing. And as a good listener, this will really build trust.

You may ask them what positive lessons they have learned in the institution. Stay away from the negatives, which would be a near endless list. In some cases they have not even thought of any positives, but if you keep asking the question, you will find that they will be able to come up with a rather long list of things that they have learned.

APPLICATION TO MENTOR

The residential phase is an important time to begin to develop the relationship. The most important factor during these weeks and months is to establish yourself as a good and genuine listener. If you succeed in that, then the post-residential phase will realize a relationship of growing trust.

Chapter 17

Avoiding Residential Manipulation

"Failure is delay but not defeat.

It is a temporary detour not a dead end street.

William Ward

AVOIDING RESIDENTIAL MANIPULATION

During the residential phase, since the mentor and the youth are still adapting and getting to know each other, there are certain behaviors to be aware of. Remember, as the adult you are always in control of the situation and not the youth. Here are some examples:

1. Youth brings up highly personal matters and for the sake of honesty and the openness you answer personal questions (such as your first sexual experience or how much money you earn). This manipulation is usually easily seen and it is important for the adult to maintain the boundary of controlling the conversation and not feel badly about not answering all questions.

2. A youth who is excessively nice or complementary may be seeking favors. Be on guard. Distinguish between a compliment and a good social skill and someone who is clearly pandering and manipulating. It is best to diffuse it with some humor by smiling and saying, "I know I don't look like Julia Roberts or Brad Pitt and it's not really necessary to discuss those things." Calling them on the behavior shows that you are alert and aware.

3. Within an institution, the youth know the rules and policies. If they ask for materials that are not allowed by policy, just tell them that you believe in going by the rules. They may ask for something that is contraband or has a monetary value such as a roll of stamps. The answer is always "no".

4. The youth tries to get you to say bad things about the staff or the administrators of the institution. This is always a no win situation. Never allow the youth to play the staff against you or other volunteers. You can be a good listener and say "I understand you don't like the food" without making any judgment that the staff intentionally enjoys serving undesirable food to the youth.

5. A youth who threatens a volunteer with physical harm if they don't get their way can be met with an immediate response "If you persist with these threats, I will be compelled to report it to the staff". Unless it stops abruptly you should terminate the visit and bring it to the attention of your program coordinator and the immediate staff in the facility.

APPLICATION TO MENTOR

Because this is a voluntary program, most youth have a desire to change and grow and appreciate the friendship that a mentor relationship brings. Occasionally some will test the limits of the new relationship by trying to manipulate. If they have been in a residential program for several months or longer, they already know the rules and are simply seeing if you are willing to bend them. The best line of defense is to hold the line, and if there has to be a "bad guy" let it be the institution's rules.

Chapter 18

Mentor/Mentee Meeting Environment

"Trust men and they will be true to you.

Treat them greatly

and they will show themselves great."

Ralph Waldo Emerson

MENTOR/MENTEE MEETING ENVIRONMENT

The locations selected for the meetings between you and the youth must be chosen carefully.

There are several criteria that you may want to consider:
- **A place free of distractions.**
- **A neutral setting.**
- **A non-threatening environment.**

Free of Distractions

A place "free from distractions" means a place where neither of you will be easily recognized nor interrupted by friends, family or acquaintances. It is far better to drive an additional 20 miles to a location than meet in a corner restaurant in the youth's neighborhood. There might be places close to your work environment but co-workers may interrupt you. Distractions more likely fall into the situation of the youth meeting friends or even former antisocial peers such as gang members. The focus of the meeting is dialog, which is both listening and talking and the more you can be free of distractions, the better.

Neutral Setting

A neutral setting is basically a place where you both can agree on, where neither has any attachments or strong feelings. The operative word here is *compromise*. The simple definition of the word *compromise* is that each party gets something they want and each gives up something. There will be no perfect location for both people, but you should, with minimal discussion, be able to find a location that is acceptable to both.

Non-Threatening

A non-threatening environment is one that will not create any stress or tension for the youth. Although not easily seen, a close association with a place that looks and feels "institutional" is an example. In the post-release phase having come out of an institution where the youth was confined anywhere from months to years, it is better to keep away from any institutional building or office setting.

Places to avoid:
- **School classroom.**
- **Youth dance club.**
- **Hospital.**
- **Office building.**
- **Church sanctuary.**

Office

Clearly you would not meet at a police station or a probation officer's building but there are many settings that can easily remind the youth of a place with they meet with a therapist, social worker or an interview room. As a mentor, you may have a nice office, but it is better to avoid the office setting. You would certainly not want to sit behind a desk and look too authoritative when you are trying to form a friendship.

Church

Although a church may be a comfortable setting for an adult mentor, the church sanctuary can be intimidating to a unchurched youth. Even a young person who has attended church with their family may feel uneasy in a setting foreign to them. As an example, those who have been raised in a high liturgical church such as an Anglican or Roman Catholic Church can be very comfortable with stained glass windows, an altar, a crucifix, and statues. But for someone who came from a Presbyterian or Bible church background, the high liturgical architecture and symbols may seem strange. Conversely, someone who is well acquainted with a liturgical church with ample artistic symbolism such as stained glass windows, statues and other artifacts will find a stark or barren sanctuary (whitewashed) in the Calvinistic style unsettling.

Obviously a Muslim may feel ill at ease in a Jewish synagogue, and a Jewish youth may feel equally uncomfortable in a mosque.

Endorsement

There is also subliminal communication that might suggest to the youth that the mentor is endorsing a particular church body or denomination by meeting there. Churches are a comfortable setting for many adults but not necessarily for youth. The trend in new churches (post-modern) is to build a special area for youth that sometimes includes video games, contemporary posters, and table games like ping pong and foosball.

An auditorium where there is rap or rock music may feel comfortable for the youth but is usually noisy, loud and quite active. This is hardly the place most adults would feel comfortable in.

House

A house is not a suggested setting either. As a mentor, you may have a beautiful home but if there is a substantial difference in the socioeconomic class between you and the youth's family, it can seem ostentatious. The youth reporting back on material possessions may seem intimidating to a poor family. Likewise, if a youth's home has been a setting for arguments and other family disruptions, that may not be the best place for a meeting. There is the possibility that someone in another room, even with the door closed, can be listening to the conversation. Even perception can stifle conversation.

School

A school classroom may also be a drawback if the youth struggled with school subjects or had confrontations with school officials. The school classroom often looks identical to the public school in an institution.

Recommended environments

Environments should be chosen through compromise but also by finding a common interest and activities that the mentor and youth can participate in together.

This is not an exclusive list but some examples of environments that can fulfill neutrality and be a non-threatening place free of distractions.

Shopping Mall

Going to the shopping mall in the off times, early in the morning or late afternoon avoids the congestion of youth traffic on a Saturday or the hustle and bustle of people coming in the early evening or lunch hour. In a mall, you and the youth can talk as you walk or you can sit down in the food court, which is mostly isolated, at a time that does not have high traffic.

The shopping mall has become a replacement of the town square, where youth "hung out" 60 years ago. It is a comfortable setting for most youth but be advised to find a shopping mall a good distance from the youth's neighborhood.

A Gymnasium

As a mentor, if you are agile and physically fit, you may want to play basketball together. This tends to work best for boys but can also work between an adult woman and a girl. You can have an energetic game and talk during rest periods. If the youth is talented, you may want to have an open ended discussion about what it would be like to be a pro-athlete and what steps the youth would take to achieve that goal. Youth tend to talk about the things that interest them, of course.

Public Park

Unlike a golf course that might interest only an adult mentor but not a youth, a public park offers several outdoor activities. You can run, walk or even bike together. The youth may not have a good bicycle, but there are many public parks where bikes can be rented. One can easily have a conversation while biking at a moderate speed. During rest periods, there are isolated park benches, still in view of the public, where the two of you can talk freely with a degree of privacy.

A Zoo

Not all youth like zoos. They may think of that location as childish, but there are many young people that like animals and aside from the public park atmosphere, you can easily talk as you walk.

There is the opportunity to ask a leading question that can result in significant revelation. The mentor can ask the youth what animal they would like to be if they could be any animal. The answer is not important; it is only the "why". As an example, someone might say they would <u>most</u> like to be an ant because it is industrious and lifts 10 times its own weight. Another person might also say they would <u>least</u> like to be an ant because they are small, insignificant and easily stepped on. The choice of the ant was not relevant. It was simply the explanation. Talking about animals is a safe way for a youth to talk about themselves without being too direct or personal. The zoo location may be a good stimulus, early in the relationship, for good conversation.

Art Museum

This may seem an unlikely location but can be a good experience. An art museum does not have an institutional look like an office building. It would be wise to pick a museum that has a combination of modern and traditional art. As an open ended question, you can ask the youth to find a painting they most like and ask why. As you listen, you will learn about their self-image. There are many young people that like art, and in institutions many youth like to draw. If they have talent, it is an area where you can affirm and motivate. Surprisingly, some young people have never set foot in an art museum. And this, while not necessarily a regular meeting place, can be a good experience.

Movie Theater

While the viewing of a movie is rather passive, talking about the characters in the movie at a small café right after the film can be a great stimulus for conversation. You should be careful not to choose a film that is overly violent or has objectionable material. As you find a movie you can both agree on, opt for the one that deals with relationships.

A Coffee Shop

There are many coffee shops like Starbucks in each community, and weather permitting, you can often sit outside. At an off peak time you will find a degree of privacy. They offer many beverages other than coffee such as iced tea and soda so both of you will have a beverage.

A Bookstore

Many young people like to express themselves in a diary or journal and may even have the potential as a writer. Going into a bookstore gives you the opportunity to buy an economical gift, perhaps a classic book that you can both read together and discuss. It could be anything from a classic like *Pilgrim's Progress* or *Tom Sawyer* to more challenging works like *Moby Dick*. The larger bookstore has a small café where, in the off peak times, there will be a degree of privacy for conversation.

APPLICATION TO MENTOR

Choosing the right location for your meetings is very important. The environment needs to be free of distractions, neutral and non-threatening. Avoid office buildings, anyplace that looks institutional, homes, or even churches. Whether bike riding, walking, playing basketball, or sitting in a coffee shop, you should be able to find a place and share an activity that you both feel comfortable with. It is important to drive a reasonable distance from the youth's neighborhood so the youth will not be distracted by friends or peers with antisocial values.

Chapter 19

Mentors Keeping Families Informed

"If you would be loved, love and be loveable."

Benjamin Franklin

MENTORS KEEPING FAMILIES INFORMED

In some states mentoring programs do not allow a mentor who visits during a residential phase to continue in the release phase. It is, however, this author's recommendation that it be the same person for the sake of continuity and consistency.

After the residential phase, it is important to keep the family informed of when and where you are meeting with the youth.

In the post-residential phase you should have developed a trust relationship with family members and good communication is both essential and courteous.

Meetings

You will need to inform a parent or guardian whether the meetings are going to be weekly or monthly and the purpose of the meetings. Simply explain that mentoring is not just a relationship but also guiding their son or daughter to make good decisions and embrace good values. Never imply that the family has poor values or are not capable of being good role models, even if that is the case.

Support

Always inform family members that you are here to assist the family as well as the youth and to strengthen healthy relationships. A struggling single mom, for instance, will appreciate that there is an adult male in a boy's life and communication will improve as a result of the mentoring relationship.

Be careful never to set up any situation in which a parent or guardian can feel threatened by the mentor relationship. Offering spectacular field trips while excluding other siblings can set up rivalry. The mentor may want to consider bringing siblings to a sports event but letting the family know that the other meeting times are for private conversations.

The Meeting Location

Always let a parent or guardian know the exact location that you are going to and whenever possible give them your cell phone number. Let the family know if you are going to be with the youth alone or if there will be other friends or family members with you, such as your spouse. It is also helpful to give the exact time that you will be together so a family member can anticipate a youth's return, especially for preparation of lunch or dinner. If the youth misleads a parent or guardian and goes to be with friends after your meeting, your communication will help the parent compare stories and give the opportunity to question where the youth was.

When (of a Meeting)

It is better when meetings are a consistent day and time whenever possible. As an example, you may meet with the youth on Saturday mornings and it will be easier for the parent or guardian to plan for the youth to be picked up or dropped off at your meeting location.

How

The "how" is simply letting them know how you will rendezvous with the youth. Will you pick them up in your car? Is the parent expected to drop them off? Or is the youth to take public transportation?

Why

Finally, the "why" specifically addresses the type of meeting, whether it is for conversation and communication, recreational, or attending a specific event.

APPLICATION TO MENTOR

Maintaining good communication with the youth's family is essential. They should never guess about a meeting time or location. It is a courtesy to the family, but it is also a safeguard for you as a mentor so that time is accounted for and the youth does not have an opportunity to manipulate a parent by telling them they were with you when they were with friends or at a party. Keeping good communication is an important part of building your relationship with a youth's family.

Chapter 20

Mentor Responsibility to the Team

"When we love, we give up the center of ourselves."

Rollo May

MENTOR RESPONSIBILITY TO THE TEAM

As a mentor, you are responsible to the team. Never act as "a lone ranger" and claim the relationship with the youth apart from the program.

You should arrive on time for all required training and seek out the program coordinator and other members of the team when you have questions. You should review this manual more than once to become familiar with all the basic requirements and expectations of a mentor. Do not hesitate to ask for help if you have any concerns or questions. That is why you are part of a team.

Monthly Report

You will be required to fill out monthly paperwork to keep track of attendance and the development of the relationship. The paperwork is important as a part of the research that will document the success of this program. It is hoped that this program can be replicated in other states as a model, and your faithfulness in doing the paperwork will help in that regard.

Building Trust

Remember that the mentor/mentee relationship is voluntary, it is one-on-one, and it thrives in an atmosphere of trust, maintaining confidentiality, and being patient and non-judgmental. If you are concerned about the development of the relationship or the youth's family, use the team, especially the program coordinator, for assistance.

APPLICATION TO MENTOR

Your sacrifice and dedication in this program is greatly appreciated, but you must remember that you have several responsibilities. You are a member of a team and must comply with all reasonable requests including paperwork, ongoing training and good communication. Do not let problems fester or develop over weeks or months but bring them to the attention of other members of the team while problems are still manageable.

Chapter 21

How a Mentor Demonstrates Interest in the Youth

"Getting people to like you is merely
the other side of liking them."

Norman Vincent Peale

HOW A MENTOR DEMONSTRATES INTEREST IN THE YOUTH

Listening

One of the easiest ways to demonstrate interest in any person is to keep good and frequent communication. All human beings appreciate a good listener. Everyone has a story to tell and the youth you work with is no exception. In some cases, they have never really had a caring adult take the time to truly listen to them. You can ask for clarification and give feedback during a conversation, but listening is a very important attribute for a functioning, mentoring relationship. To listen you have to be attentive. This means eye contact, never looking bored and showing that you are listening through body language, such as nodding.

Humor

Within conversation it is perfectly acceptable to have humor. As an example, healthy marriages have humor. This simply means that you are not taking yourself too seriously and you realize there are things you can laugh about in yourself. Never let the humor be aimed at other people, at their physical characteristics or the weaknesses of other members of the team, or the youth's parents or teachers. Model respect for the youth, and keep humor away from mocking or ridicule.

Common Interests

Youth will believe that you care about them as you go out of your way to find common interests. If you like the symphony and the youth does not, dragging them to the symphony every month is not going to help build the relationship. Conversely, you do not have to go to a rock concert. But you will be able to find many activities that are a good compromise and show that you are making an effort.

There are times when small, brief communication can be just as effective; a quick postcard with an encouraging note or writing a short letter that affirms and encourages. Many times the youth will keep these and reread them. No harm is ever done by showing interest in what the youth thinks, feels, and does.

APPLICATION TO MENTOR

A mentor best shows interest by talking about what interests the youth, not the adult. Be careful not to dominate conversation. Listening shows interest. Asking questions that cannot be answered by a simple "yes" or "no" open youth to sharing their interests.

Chapter 22

Cultural Differences

"Love focuses on a present relationship
while moving forward toward a future goal."

Williams Hiemstra

CULTURAL DIFFERENCES

A mentor should be sensitive to the race and ethnicity of the youth. They may come from a different part of town, socio-economically, often referred to as "the wrong side of the tracks." They may be poor, they made be middle class, or even wealthy. Generally the youth who are in a juvenile justice facility come from a middle or a lower socio-economic range.

Their parents frequently do not have advanced degrees such as college or graduate studies, and sometimes not high school.

A youth may be embarrassed that a parent speaks little or no English. It is natural during this period that ethnic groups stay together and are not only isolated geographically and linguistically, but youth are attracted to an ethnic gang, as an example. This causes natural rivalries and prejudice, which go back historically to early America, if not centuries, in civilization.

Even among the "mainstream students" who have not violated laws, within the school they categorize themselves into sub-groups; the jocks, the nerds, the preps, and so forth. The parable of the Good Samaritan, as found in Luke 17:11-19, is a good story to share with youth as it deals with someone serving and helping a victim of another culture. Within the biblical story it is the person least likely to help who does so. You can tell the story in a contemporary version by changing the cultures to fit the ethnicity of the youth and his neighborhood. As an example, when would a wealthy white suburbanite help a poor injured Hispanic?

APPLICATION TO MENTOR

Most important for the mentor is to take serious culture differences and never make light of them. There is also the danger of making it a bigger issue and putting it in the forefront. As an example, with a youth from a Mexican background you would naturally not stress how much you like tacos, just as you would not highlight your love of boiled potatoes for someone who is Irish or spaghetti for someone who is Italian. Learn what the youth and his family most like about their ethnic background and always stress positives. Stay away from any cultural stereotypes and definitely avoid any nicknames that youth are apt to give to other races or ethnic groups.

Chapter 23

The Effects of Culture

"Religious words have value
to the child only as experience in the home
gives them meaning."

John Drescher

THE EFFECTS OF CULTURE ON YOUTH

The American culture is full of opportunities and dangers for youth are very different from the world in which most adult mentors grew up.

A mentor must maintain generational boundaries, which means never act like a "buddy" or a teenager just to identify with a youth. It is far better to ask them why they enjoy a rap artist than to mimic the lyrics yourself or watch MTV as if preparing for a mentor exam.

If you look at teen magazines such as *J-14, Teen People's Magazine* and others, you will see many beautiful young people like Lindsay Lohan, Hillary Duff, the sisters Jessica and Ashley Simpson, as well as rapper 50 Cent, Nick Carter and Jesse McCartney. Aside from the magazines talking about beauty, fame and putting movie stars and rock stars on pedestals, you need not look closely to realize that the photos are all taken under controlled circumstances. Professional photographers carefully work with the light. The hairstylist tries to get every hair in place. And both male and female have makeup. But in addition, photographers will spend much time retouching the photographs. Their purpose is to hide every imperfection. If you were to meet some of the young rock stars and movie stars outside of the photographic studio, you would find the same blemishes, scars and imperfections that everyone else has. But the magazines are selling a product of perfection, which is, of course, impossible to reach. Even the stories that accompany the young lives are often exaggerated if not totally fictitious. Behind all the attention and autograph seeking fans some of these people may still suffer isolation, loneliness and even depression if their values are superficial.

As a mentor, you are most successful when you are simply yourself with your unique history and life experiences. But an understanding of the influence of culture on youth will help you understand the stress and the dangers that many youth face.

Technology

Most teens act as if CDs, DVDs, personal computers and cell phones always existed. As adults we know these are new technologies, and in some cases it is difficult for us to even play catch up. While the computer has revolutionized homework by searching the Internet with intriguing questions, we also know there are the dangers of pornography, chat rooms and instant messaging that can socially isolate a teen from the group. Today's teenagers are surrounded with visual and auditory stimulation. Some seem glued to a CD player or an Ipod. Television, movies and many lyrics are filled with violence and graphic depictions of violent crimes.

Messages

A popular video game is Grand Theft Auto played on a Play Station 2. It has graphic images of people car-jacking, killing and kidnapping victims. One of the top singles by rap artist 50 Cent is *Candy Shop*. It may sound tame but it is a metaphor for oral sex, which has become a growing behavior in many middle schools.

You will not be able to remove the influence of culture by simply condemning it. As a mentor it is far better to listen to why youth are attracted to a particular artist or why they enjoyed a particular movie as you try to see the world through their eyes.

After several months in the mentor relationship, youth will know your standards and values; you need not give lectures or preach about those parts of the culture (music, fashion, movies) that you object to. They already know.

Communication

By keeping the door of communication open, by being a good listener, you encourage the youth to be self-analytical. That simply means many will come to the decision themselves that the values of a particular movie, TV program or music is negative and it is better when they choose alternatives.

Lasting change will come through the youth making good decisions. And they will make more good decisions by learning from their bad decisions.

You are a guide in the process, but it is your affirmation, your encouragement and the values of your life that will most influence them.

APPLICATION FOR MENTOR

Although there are parts of a teen's culture, such as their choice of music, television and movies that you may object to, keep the lines of communication open and listen to why they enjoy or value them. Sometimes it is as simple as peer pressure. With the vast amount of visual and auditory stimulation in their life, you know they also need to read as part of their education. As their mentor, you can be a signpost in the cultural wilderness of a youth's life.

Chapter 24

When a Youth Has a Parent in Prison

"Those who deserve love the least
need it the most."

Anonymous

WHEN A YOUTH HAS A PARENT IN PRISON

There are two million children between the ages of five and eighteen who have one parent in prison.

Half of the parents are African American, 49.4%, with many being fathers (93%). Frequently, youth in a state juvenile justice facility have had or presently have one parent incarcerated, and they currently have a sibling or a close relative in jail or prison.

There are several ways in which that can have a bad effect, especially on the self-esteem of the youth you work with as a mentor.

Here are some examples:

- **Family Curse**

  Some youth may come to think of their potential imprisonment as inevitability or even a family curse, a type of self-fulfilling prophecy, and as a result set out to prove their "inherited" tendencies by law violative behaviors.

- **Emotional**

  Having a parent incarcerated is a social stigma. Many youth will hide the fact or even lie about where their parent is. They are afraid of being ridiculed by their peers and being looked down upon by their teachers. It is an emotional burden.

- **Destiny**

  Youth who have a parent in prison may adapt a false notion of a self-fulfilling prophecy, as mentioned above, because a parent was in prison they are destined to lead a criminal life or be in an adult prison themselves. As a mentor you are in a strategic position to break that negative thinking and let them know that they are capable of good choices they make will send them in a different direction.

- **Financial**

  Having a parent in prison creates several burdens on a family. Clearly some of them are financial. Sometimes transportation to the prison is a long journey and costly. Also long distance phone calls will add up if the prison is far away. And for a "single" mom visiting her husband, that will weigh on the family's economy. Often the cost of legal defense has also drained the family of resources and a mom may be going to work for the first time.

- **Movement**

  Some of the youth in this mentoring program have had multiple caregivers, and this can lead to a youth feeling instability. During the incarceration of a parent they may have lived with a grandparent or an aunt or an uncle. Some of these youth have gone from one shelter care facility to another or a halfway house because of their entrance into the juvenile court system, juvenile detention and a residential placement. While all of these people and institutions have done their best to provide structure for the youth, it still has the possible effect of causing the child to not feel the support of a particular caring adult.

APPLICATION TO MENTOR

The number of incarcerated moms (females) who have children has risen dramatically, 60% of the mothers that are incarcerated live at least 100 miles away from their children. When a mother is incarcerated 79% of the children are placed with other family members. As a mentor you will learn this information about a parent or sibling who is incarcerated. Be a good listener. Discover how this has affected the youth, especially listening for indications of fear of rejection, shame, embarrassment and other symptoms of stress. As the relationship you have with the youth grows, one of the best ways to overcome the fear of rejection and shame that youth carry by having an incarcerated parent is to facilitate positive communication with the incarcerated parent. As a mentor, you can help create healing between the youth and that parent, especially if the youth resents or has anger toward the parent. You can facilitate this by reviewing good letters that express forgiveness, accompany them to visit the parent in an institution if policy allows, and helping the parent realize that although they are policy allows, and helping the parent realize that although they are incarcerated they can still encourage the youth through phone calls and letters since they never stop being a parent. A mentor cannot undo the past but can help the youth face the challenges and burdens of an incarcerated parent with optimism and break any notion that it is a prophecy for their own future.

Chapter 25

Youth Anxiety

"Love does not parade the imperfections of others
or taunt people for their weaknesses.
Rather love seeks to understand others
– the imperfections and weaknesses."

Anonymous

YOUTH ANXIETY

As a mentor, you are aware of the role of anxiety in adult life. But it is a larger factor for teens. Anxiety, unlike fear, does not always have a specific source. The danger may be imaginary. Aside from the lack of freedom and mobility that the teen has had in a residential facility (a consequence of their antisocial behavior), they may fear a return to a neighborhood fraught with temptations from anti-social peers. The world is a scary place for many youth. When they were young they saw the mass destruction of the Oklahoma City bombing and images of the World Trade Towers collapsing in New York City. That is a defining moment as was the sinking ships at Pearl Harbor for their grandparents. Political tensions and the constant threats of international terrorism affect youth. They may ask themselves, how can they manage their own lives when the adults are having difficulty managing their countries? For a young person who is still forming their worldview, the world can seem like an out of control place. They are still trying to find their role. Religious beliefs can be very important for a teen. They need to believe in a God that is all-powerful and is in control even when parts of the world appear out of control.

APPLICATION TO MENTOR

For the mentor, understand that the anxiety that is naturally felt by both the period of adolescence and a reaction to what can easily be perceived as a threatening world will often show itself behaviorally. The youth you are working with may have turned to drugs or alcohol in the past to subdue anxiety. Being a good listener helps, and part of listening is empathy. Words like "I understand," nodding your head, leaning forward in your chair always indicate you are interested in what the young person is saying. Point out the positive things you see in the youth. Thousands of people opened their homes to those who lost homes in the aftermath of Hurricane Katrina. There is always good if you look for it. Show how it is possible to live in a world of tension and still find happiness through worthy goals.

Chapter 26

Consumerism and Youth

"Love is freely giving,
expecting nothing in return."

Mary Carson

CONSUMERISM AND YOUTH

Consumerism is closely linked with marketing and advertising in America. It often preys on young people by convincing them that something they want is a need. Advertising wants young people to become active consumers.

Most adults have learned to regulate the use of credit cards, pay bills on time, and not purchase every latest fad or fashion. But youth are still impressionable and impulsive. They seek instant gratification and find it difficult to save their money over a long period and then buy an item when they have sufficient funds.

The youth that you work with came out of moderate, medium, or high-level facilities. At the point they entered the juvenile justice system they wore a uniform in detention and probably uniform clothing in a facility. You can assume they did not like the conformity of being in an institution. Any questioning, during the residential phase, about their attire would meet with strong objections. This is more because the uniform or clothing of an institution is not optional but mandatory. And yet there is a paradox or contradiction. If you asked youth if they would want to wear a uniform when they return home, they would easily say no. But go to any public school and watch how quickly the changing fashions are adapted.

Peer Pressure

Youth basically dress alike. When a hairstyle changes, it changes across the board. Whether it is short or long, spiked or colored, they will imitate each other for the sake of conformity. Sneakers, jeans, and t-shirts have become a traditional American teenage uniform. Although only adopted by a minority at first, surfers used flip-flops or ghetto kids had sagging pants and it soon created a wave of conformity and was adopted nationwide.

Teenagers want to fit in. They want to be a part of a group. The youth you work with became part of a sub-group, often deviant and antisocial because of the crimes they engaged in, including the use of illegal drugs.

Conformity

That need for conformity still exists. As a mentor you can redirect them toward healthy achievement. By modeling, you can help them move from anger to patience and self-control. You can help them turn away from antisocial peers and form productive goals such as completing an education, obtaining a good job, acquiring vocational skills, or going to college.

Self-Image

One of the dangers of consumerism is that the child will associate self-esteem with possessing material things. Ipods become a fashion accessory just as designer jeans and high priced sneakers are considered necessary. Youth are attracted to labels that often have high price tags. There is nothing intrinsically evil about Nintendo, Play Station 2, TSP or girls whose conception of beauty comes from magazines like *Cosmo, Vogue* and *Thirteen.*

APPLICATION FOR MENTOR

As a responsible adult you might tell youth about a time in your life where the use of credit was excessive. By affirming and encouraging the youth you are telling them that their value comes from who they are as a person, not what they own, what they buy or what they wear. When you or someone who is part of an accountability team helps them with life skills such as balancing a checkbook and saving earned money, they will hopefully begin to balance the false messages from advertising with the real messages of what they really need as opposed to what they want. Love and acceptance is greater then money and possessions.

Chapter 27

Strengthening a Youth's Sense of Community

"Love has hands to help others.

It has feet to hasten to the poor and needy.

It has eyes to see misery and want.

It has ears to hear the sights and sorrows of men.

This is what love looks like."

Augustine

STRENGTHING A YOUTH'S SENSE OF COMMUNITY

For high-risk youth who come from a fragmented or dysfunctional family, many have not experienced genuine community; an environment where people are bonded by like values, show mutual respect, and attend to those in need.

As adults, we have experienced "community" on many levels. Some mentors belong to fraternal organizations like the Rotary Club, Kiwanis, or the Lion's Club. Others are veterans of wars and have attended reunions over the years. Those in a church experience community with a group of like-minded people.

Experience

The sociology of religion has shown that many youth have an intense hunger to experience something that validates God's existence. Experiencing genuine community is to be part of a group of people that not only have common and shared beliefs, but serve and support one another. Youth can begin to see how important living in an atmosphere of mutual respect is.

Golden Rule

The basis of our American society is the "Golden Rule". Simply stated "doing for others what you would want done for you."

Of course, with the youth's past criminal activities, they have violated this important rule of society. Some have stolen property. They may have hurt someone physically or damaged or destroyed property. But that past does not make them a career criminal or set a pattern of behavior for life.

As a mentor, you have an opportunity to teach them through demonstration what community is about. Acts of service, such as cleaning a vacant lot or planting flowers in a public park are not only a public service but might even be a form of restitution. You can do these projects together.

Restitution

Restitution, which is a biblical concept, is not about making the victim whole. It is as much about teaching the offender the value of giving back to individuals and the community. You may want to encourage your mentee to become involved in Teen Court. In Teen Court, youth practice deciding and adjudicating minor transgressions through peer review. It is a national movement.

Good Citizen

Involvement in student government in school is another way youth can experience democracy in action. They will learn the value of representation and the importance of the individual vote. Democracy is a community value.

Helping those less fortunate in the community will demonstrate to youth that we are all connected and we all can grow together.

Many adults know that a sense of community has been lost in neighborhoods today, where neighbors hardly know each other. Many years ago people on the same block were often related. You could easily walk across the street to borrow a cup of sugar or to deliver leftovers. Today we are more isolated as communities.

As a mentor, becoming involved in local government or a community-watch program can be a significant teaching lesson for the young person you are working with. As he or she watches your dedication to the community, this will give them a good model.

APPLICATION TO MENTOR

Many at-risk and high-risk youth have not experienced a sense of community. As a mentor you have a great opportunity to introduce them to civic groups and the church and experience people who care about each other and serve one another. To the degree that you are involved in your community as an individual, you will be able to teach many important and sound principles to the youth.

Here are suggested activities between the mentor and mentee that can build the youth's sense of community.

1. Together you can help build a house for someone below the poverty level through an organization like Habitat for Humanity. The amount of the physical work is usually proportionate to a person's age and skill. At the same time, a youth can develop a useful skill that can be used in the future.

2. Together you can locate an older person in the community, perhaps a widow, who needs some yard work or perhaps the restoration of some shingles that have blown off. These people can be located through a local church or it may be as simple as driving down the block and observing a house that has some physical needs.

    It is beneficial for the young person to come in contact with people in different age groups and do something sacrificial that helps someone in the community that ordinarily cannot help themselves.

3. Together you can volunteer at a homeless shelter or a soup kitchen through a local Salvation Army facility. This project can take one day or several hours and incorporates the notion of service. Together you can stand in a food line and hand out food, help prepare the food, or gather and distribute clothing. By coming in contact with homeless people, once again the youth is exposed to needs in the community and begins to discover his or her greater role within the community.

4. Together the mentor and mentee may visit a nursing home. There are many shut-ins in their homes who receive Meals-on-Wheels but rarely get out. The exercise here can be anything from a visitation to bringing a pet, which many elderly people appreciate, or simply listening to a story about the past. This, once again, gives the youth a sense of generational continuity.

5. Together the mentor and mentee can visit a hospital or hospice. The reality of death and dying is not ordinarily in the forefront of an

adolescent's thoughts. But visiting someone who may be dying of HIV/AIDS or lung cancer as a result of smoking can also have a therapeutic effect without the need for moralizing or preaching.

6. Together the mentor and mentee can raise money for charity. There are many creative ways this can be done that also incorporate an activity. As an example, together they can be in a marathon bike race and receive so many dollars per mile, which can be applied to the American Cancer Society, The Heart Foundation, Muscular Dystrophy Association or the American Diabetic Association, to name a few.

    Another way to raise money for a charity would be a walk-a-thon in which case individuals would sponsor both the mentor and the mentee and the proceeds would again go to charity. This has a dual purpose. Time is spent in the relationship in a physical activity, but there is also the altruistic purpose of contributing toward the greater good.

7. The mentor and the youth can engage in a relief project. As an example: strong hurricane winds in a part of Florida may result in a church team visiting that site for the purpose of bringing people water, supplies and helping to clean up. Since Florida is a state that frequently has hurricane damage, these relief efforts may be sporadic but should they occur, they will present a good opportunity for the mentor and the mentee to work together toward giving back to the community.

SUMMARY

All of these activities are designed to help the youth see the bigger picture of what living in a community is about.

As they begin to understand that they can make sacrifices for the benefit of other people and they can be a servant to others, they learn valuable lessons about how people are linked together and how needs can be met through the kindness and volunteerism of individuals.

The youth may not always see the sacrifices the mentor is making, but by being involved in worthy projects may come to even appreciate the mentoring program more.

Projects like these are the best way to convey what a church community is about. Many young people think of the church as a building and then think of a set of rules and regulations. When faith communities are functioning, most of their ministry is outside the walls of the building. The best way to introduce a young person to a faith community is through service. There are many churches across America where service to those less fortunate is an ongoing activity, and both the mentor and the mentee will find many opportunities.

Building a Church Support
Group for Youth

"A small boy was perceptive when he looked up at the
stained glass windows in a church and said,
'A saint is a person that light shines through."
Richard Ruble

BUILDING A CHURCH SUPPORT GROUP FOR YOUTH

Mentors should not feel that they have to provide for every need the youth has. Some youth, more than others, will need guidance in social skills, others in life skills and a myriad of other areas. Within your church or community group you may be able to find other caring adults who can form a team. This team is best called an "accountability team" and does not rival the mentoring team that is assisting you. By sharing responsibilities, as a mentor you can focus on developing your relationship and your listening skills while others provide practical assistance.

Here are some examples of what an accountability team can do.

Tutoring

There will be at least one subject in which the youth may struggle or need assistance. There might easily be people in your church (or community group) who are willing to tutor the youth in basic English skills, science or math. As a mentor you can provide tutoring in a specific area but having a tutor be a part of the accountability team frees you for relationship building.

Life Skills

From your own life, there are many lessons that you will teach the youth. There are, however, some specific life skills that others can assist with. Learning how to cook, managing a household budget, balancing a checkbook, especially as a young person moves toward emancipation or independence, these life skills can be vital. Also, learning how to fill out a job application and even doing role-play of a job interview can be a very practical and useful lesson for youth. You may do this yourself as a mentor but may seek the assistance of someone in your church or community group.

Social Skills

Much of your relationship as a mentor/mentee is that of a role model. They will observe your manners, your self-control, and how you handle your life responsibilities. You can work with the parents or guardian in non-threatening discussions about hygiene, use of makeup and appropriate fashion. Many young girls wear inappropriate clothing to the mall. Working with the parents or with a member of an accountability team can help provide guidance. Many young people, while trying to fit in with their peers may not understand how a pierced tongue or eyebrow, purple spiked hair or a homemade tattoo on the face or neck could even subconsciously affect them during a job interview.

Life Skills

Teaching them how to drive (for those who do not have a license) can be very important for a young person. The patience and time taken will be greatly appreciated by the teen, and by a single mom without a car.

APPLICATON FOR MENTOR

As a mentor, you may find other caring adults in your church or community group who can be part of an accountability team for the youth. They can help with life and social skills, and as a tutor. By sharing responsibilities with others, as a mentor you can focus on developing a relationship and your listening skills.

You are the adult and the two of you are never buddies. You are there because you have life experiences and in most cases the stability of many years of marriage, raising children, going to college, paying taxes, going to work, voting, serving on jury duty, and belonging to a church or a fraternal organization. What you may consider your normal life, your day-in and day-out living, is what is most valuable for your mentee. Like most of us you have made poor decisions in life, but you have also made far more good decisions. While you may not think as the youth does, you can help adapt your wisdom and life experiences to their situation whenever possible.

Chapter 29

Affirming Youth

"When we love another truly,

he docs not have to measure up.

We accept and love him as he is."

Wynne Gillis

AFFIRMING THE YOUTH

Nothing is more frustrating than people who judge us, who tell us what we ought to be and how we ought to act. Only when a person comes to the realization that they need to change will the change really take place. So whenever possible, do not send letters that are preachy or judgmental. Do not give unsolicited advice during conversations. Showing interest gets positive results in a non-judgmental environment.

Advice

Feel free to ask for their opinions even when you disagree. That is hard for some adults. They think what young people want is advice. But think about it. Do you like unsolicited advice? Not really. You only accept advice when you ask for it or when it comes from someone you genuinely trust.

Humility

As you grow in the relationship with the youth it is perfectly acceptable for you to apologize to the youth when you have made a mistake. This shows that you are a humble and big person and will go a long way in developing the relationship.

Encouragement

You can demonstrate interest in the youth by allowing the conversation to be controlled by the youth occasionally. Always honestly answer questions but feel free to have boundaries and not react to questions you feel are too personal or invasive. Your openness will be appreciated.

You cannot praise someone too much unless it is phony. The youth will always know what they have done well and what their limitations are. As an example, you would not tell somebody having written a poem, "That is the greatest poem ever written." But you can tell them that they are a potential Keats or Frost and point out all the things in the poem you liked. Many youth like to express themselves in writing. When you read their story, do not comment on typos and bad grammar. Look at all the positives and creativity of the story and encourage them in that. Let the tutor work on grammar and help with spelling. There is no greater tool in your human arsenal as a mentor than the power of encouragement.

Interest

When you ask for a young person's opinion, simply be a good listener. It does not mean you agree with their opinions about the world, politics, or culture. It simply means that you are taking the time to hear how they see the world and how they interpret it. That demonstrates interest. Interest and caring are synonymous. They will know you care because you are giving up your time. And youth know that time is valuable for adults.

Emotional growth for a 15 or 16-year-old is not going to be in leaps and bounds. Studies at the Harvard Medical School show that the portions of the brain that regulate impulse control, reasoning and decision-making are not fully formed until the age of 20. There is empirical data that shows there is no replacement for good old-fashioned "time". They will eventually grow up and grow out of bad behaviors. And as a mentor, you are the stable force, the anchor in their life, the link between the residential and the community phase.

APPLICATION TO MENTOR

The greatest sacrifice you make is giving your time to a young person that needs direction. There are many ways you can show that you care but the greatest is by listening, affirming and encouraging. You will always be able to find something good in the young person you work with and to focus on that rather than mistakes. That will send a very positive message.

As a mentor, you share your personality; the sum of your thoughts, opinions, views, and even spiritual beliefs. If you are in a faith community, you will want to gradually expose youth to your beliefs. Never do this in a preachy or dogmatic way. Let them see that your faith is real and their own will develop on its own course. Mentors who are not in a church can still show respect for the spiritual sensitivity and sense of wonder that a youth has about the purpose of their life and why they are here.

Faith is more than a list of commandments and "do's and don'ts". It is an acknowledgment that our life has value, and we are part of a bigger plan. A mentor is not interested only in a mind but a whole person, which includes the spiritual. Remember to listen, affirm and encourage in every meeting with the youth.

Chapter 30

Positive Styles of Communication with Youth

"Kindness is the language which the deaf can hear
and the blind can see."

Mark Twain

POSITIVE STYLES OF COMMUNICATION WITH YOUTH

Communication is not just verbal, but it also involves body language.

Body Language

Eye contact is always important when talking or listening to a youth. But do not confuse a hard stare, which can be intimidating, with direct eye contact. It is certainly okay to blink and to look away from time to time. But when people persist in looking at walls or ceilings, it gives the subtle, almost unconscious message that they are distracted and not giving youth full attention.

Tactful

Good communication always involves honesty, but that never means throwing out tact. Words should be measured carefully and always be non-judgmental. It is far better to listen than to speak, to keep the lines of communication open.

Open Questions

As a mentor you will want your relationship to grow to the point that the youth will discuss almost any subject, including suicidal feelings, depression, or doubts about their faith. Should the youth fundamentally disagree with your value system, it is very tempting to correct them immediately. But it is far better to ask questions like, "Why do you believe that?" Phrases like, "I think you are wrong," only puts up a wall or a barrier. Questions like, "Why do you believe that?" leaves the door open for conversation and dialog.

As a mentor, one of your goals is building self-esteem. Teenagers frequently have self-doubt and worry about their self worth. Allowing them to share their feelings in a non-judgmental atmosphere is very healthy.

Smiles and a relaxed posture, even leaning in with your body, all have a positive, unwritten message. Folding arms tightly across the chest or frowning, although not intending to be negative, can send a negative message. Your body language speaks.

Differences Are Okay

Since no two people are alike, you as a mentor and your youth will have many differences. For example, you might both like chicken, but you may like it cooked differently. One may like it fried, another baked, and still another barbequed. And, people are not hungry for chicken at the same time. So you will naturally have differences in music and movies, too. Sometimes you will be able to compromise. You may not like rap music, but you can ask the youth who their favorite artists are, and ask them what lyrics they like and why. You will also have an opportunity to expose them to good literature, perhaps Mark Twain's *Tom Sawyer* or Paul Bunyan's *Pilgrim's Progress*.

Part of the communication process is both listening and educating through empathy and patience. As your relationship grows, and that is the goal, trust will build. And as trust builds, each will feel not threatened and will be able to share more deeply.

Transparency

Even though you are older and have more life experience as a mentor, you do not have to hide your defects. You can naturally and slowly reveal them as opportunity arises, using teaching lessons to explain how you learned from your mistakes and bad decisions. In terms of communication, transparency will then open the door to helping the youth reveal and learn from their mistakes and bad decisions.

A mentor should also help the youth to engage in good communication, which means avoiding any forms of manipulation. The best communication is always honesty. People say what they mean in an atmosphere that is not critical and non-judgmental.

APPLICATION TO MENTOR

As a mentor your sincerity and caring will naturally express itself through your facial expressions and body language. If you focus on statements that encourage and are affirming, you will always help the relationship to grow. You as a mentor and the mentee are different people, but you will be able to find much common ground as the relationship develops. Keep communication empathetic and honest.

Chapter 31

Avoiding Poor Communication

"Failure is an event, never a person."

William Brown

AVOIDING POOR COMMUNICATION

Poor communication can be summed up as any style of talking or listening that is critical, judgmental, blaming or seeks to change the subject by being irrelevant.

Poor communication is basically dishonest. It has an ulterior motive of judging or blaming, and it often has at the heart some form of manipulation of the other person.

It is rare that the mentor will communicate poorly, but it is important to be aware that the youth may engage in poor communication. These may be bad, old habits. You can help to correct and reestablish good communication.

Placate

Placate is a fancy word for trying to manipulate someone. Some youth have manipulative parents and even peers who manipulate, and it has become both a learned behavior and a habit. An important part of the mentoring relationship is to help them become a good, honest communicator.

Total Agreement

One of the ways you can spot manipulative communication is when a youth agrees with you one hundred percent on everything. That would be rare in life as it would be in the mentoring relationship. It is a "red flag". People are not alike and naturally will disagree on something. You may notice the youth becoming a weathervane by talking to you as a "yes" man and accepting all criticism immediately. You may want to dig a little deeper and tell them, "You don't have to please me. A part of our relationship is being real and honest."

Simplicity

As a mentor, you may have a good education, but always talk in simple language considering that many of these youth function at a third grade reading level. Do not intellectualize your conversations. Avoid big words and long paragraphs with lots of points. Sometimes people who intellectualize are trying to maintain control. You are not in any contest with the youth, and you have no reason to take anything personal. Let youth express themselves in the way that they need to. As a mentor, keep your points brief so you will allow youth to react and to speak. Just because someone appears to be listening, does not mean they hear us, especially if we are sermonizing or preaching.

Blaming

Another form of communication to avoid and to help youth with is "blaming". Quite often youth in a residential program have adapted (occasionally from psychologists) a style of blaming problems on parents and society in general, which takes the responsibility off of themselves. Never allow a youth to blame you for their own problems, and conversely do not blame them for the relationship not developing quickly. Blaming always makes people defensive and it never is a constructive tool for problem solving.

Unconditional acceptance simply means that you will not let any slip of the tongue or judgmental comment from the youth erode or destroy the relationship. By modeling good communication skills and keeping control of your thoughts and your tongue, even if the youth slips with an expletive or engages in any form of name-calling or blaming, you can always model appropriate communication.

APPLICATION TO MENTOR

As a mentor you will always strive to be honest and clear. Understanding dysfunctional communication will help you spot it in the youth you work with. While we think of dishonesty as the worse form of communication (and certainly it is improper), placating or having the youth manipulate you through trying to please you can, in the long term, be just as harmful. Use your intuition and common sense to guide you. Trust is earned not inherited with the relationship.

Chapter 32

What is a Healthy Family?

"A real friend is one who helps us think our best thoughts,
to do our noblest deeds and to be our finest selves."

Anonymous

WHAT IS A HEALTHY FAMILY?

As a mentor you are in a unique position not only to help a youth but their family as well. Mentors can assist in creating a healthy family.

Many families today, especially the families of the boys and girls who have been in the juvenile justice system are anything but traditional. Some families are blended, some broken, and some youth have lived with multiple caregivers.

Many adult mentors were raised in traditional families with a mother and father. Perhaps only your father worked and your mother stayed at home to raise the children. Sometimes grandparents lived in the same home or on the same block. Youth today have had different experiences.

We have all heard of the term "dysfunctional family." Simplified it means that the concept of a mother, father and children living together, often called the "nuclear family," is often absent.

Many of the youth in the mentoring program have no father or a father who is physically or emotionally distant. You may know that 70% of mothers with children ages 6 to 17 are in the workplace creating what has become known as "latch-key children," which means children who let themselves in their house with their own key after school with considerable time without supervision.

Most juvenile crime takes place between the hours of 3:30 and 6:00 p.m. and not on Friday or Saturday nights as most would guess. That is a time in which, without supervision, many teenagers are involved with gang activity, illegal drug usage, spend time with antisocial peers, or play violent video games like Grand Theft Auto.

Rather than using the term "normal family" it is far better to use the term "healthy family," which implies mutual respect, love and nurturing.

As a mentor, you can form a unique bond with parents. A single mom often needs emotional support. As a mentor you are never in competition with parents or with the family. A mentor is not a substitute parent, nor is your relationship (or your family's) with the youth a substitute family.

In your mentor conversations with the youth, always be supportive of a parent's discipline and boundary setting. If you disagree with a parent's discipline, always talk with the parent in private and never get trapped in the middle, siding with the parent or the youth.

As a mentor, you can help support a healthy family, by encouraging good communication, parental listening, and times in which the parent (or parents) engage in activities with the youth and plan small getaways or vacations.

Psychologists have found that having one meal together each day during which time parents or guardians listen to the youth, advances toward a healthy family.

No parents are perfect, just as no child is perfect. Most parents learn their skills from watching their own parents, and they are inclined to repeat the mistakes of their own parents, as well. Just as you, as a mentor, may engage in recreational activities with a youth, encourage the parent or guardian to find common interests also, such as biking, swimming or camping that will create bonds with their child.

If you discover that a parent is battling their own problems, including uncontrolled anger, excessive use of alcohol or the use of illegal drugs, encourage them to seek help. A parent models behaviors not by lecturing but by lifestyle. While your chief responsibility is to the youth, anything you can do to assist the family will help stabilize the youth and lead to a brighter future.

Encourage the young person you are working with to respect their parents and to never treat their home like a hotel. In a hotel other people do laundry, cook and pick up clothes, but in a family there are shared responsibilities. Encourage the young person to straighten their room, pick up their clothes, wash dishes or put them in a dishwasher, mow the lawn, and engage in other reasonable chores that show they care about their parent or guardian, and are willing to share responsibilities.

The good news is that dysfunctional families can become healthy families with guidance.

APPLICATION FOR MENTOR

As a mentor you are in a unique position to support the formation of a healthy family by helping a parent maintain generational boundaries and listen in a non-judgmental manner to their child. Encourage the youth to share responsibilities in the house such as cleaning their room, helping with laundry, cooking, washing dishes and mowing lawns. As a mentor you never want to become a substitute for a parent but in a kind way encourage mutual respect and be an encourager of both the parents and the youth.

Chapter 33

Mentor's Guide Regarding
Family Discipline

"Spare the rod and spoil the child, that is true,

but beside the rod keep an apple

to give him when he has done well."

Martin Luther

MENTOR'S GUIDE REGARDING FAMILY DISCIPLINE

Discipline is often seen as a negative behavior. A youth may remember spankings as a child as punishment, but discipline really means a parent caring enough to enforce reasonable structure and limitations for the good of their son or daughter.

One of the ways in which you, the mentor, can help parents is to show them how they can discipline in an appropriate and effective way by withholding something the child values, such as TV, music, use of computer or Ipod, and avoid corporal punishment, which is not effective with teenagers.

A mentor can help teach the parents to be fair, not to overreact to behaviors or treat one child different from another.

Since as a mentor you help to strengthen the youth's family, you can show the parent how to take a "time-out," not for the child but for themselves. It may be a long walk or sitting on a park bench. The parent can simply give themselves and their child time to cool down, then come together to talk and listen when everyone is calm.

As a mentor, you can also help the parents not engage in name-calling or profanity. By staying calm in every situation, as a mentor, you show them how it is possible to relieve stress by taking a deep breath or going for a walk and diffusing conflict. Your most important teaching role is what you model.

A mentor can also help parents stay parents by what is called "maintaining generational boundaries". Parents should never bribe children with gifts or give them money for chores when they should be expected as part of household responsibility.

As a mentor, you can help parents form agreements between their son or daughter in writing. A short contract, which you can review, can address issues like homework, arriving on time for a curfew, consequences for coming home late, or not performing expected chores like picking up clothes and keeping their room clean.

Over the years, some parents develop poor disciplining habits. As a mentor you can help re-educate parents. Guide the parent to never discipline with shame. Help the parents create a home environment of mutual respect. As an example, a parent may not like the rap music their child listens to, but as a compromise the youth can wear earphones and not use loud speakers. The parent still has the right to say no and keep objectionable material such as violent lyrics and videos out of the household.

APPLICATION TO MENTOR

As a mentor you have a great opportunity to help strengthen the youth's family. These are many practical ways you can help parents contract with their children for reasonable goals and expectations. By teaching both the youth and parents to talk and work out problems in a calm manner, you are helping the family grow.

Chapter 34

Youth's Thoughts of Suicide

"There is a way that seems right to a person
but eventually it ends in death."

Proverbs 16:25

YOUTH'S THOUGHTS OF SUICIDE

There is probably no more challenging behavior or symptoms that a mentor has to be aware of than the possibility of a young person taking their own life. In America, one teen attempts suicide every minute. The actual number of those that succeed comes to 6,500 young lives that end tragically each year. Seldom counted are the high-risk behaviors that in a sense are suicidal but are usually not counted, including drinking and driving, binge drinking, and experimentation with drugs.

If your mentee has had any history of suicide attempts or threats, the program coordinator will disclose this to you when the relationship begins.

There are some signs and symptoms that one can look for. Depression is usually a prelude to suicide. You do not have to be a clinical psychologist to use intuition and good common sense. Keep in mind that a youth's suicidal thinking will not always result in overt words. A young person does not have to tell you "I'm going to kill myself" but may be sending other signals by words like "I feel just like ending it all."

In most cases, symptoms are observable. Obvious, would be a youth obsessed with the subject of death. If they have had a close friend or relative die recently, that will be a natural part of any conversation, but not ordinarily on a week-by-week basis. They may ask about what happens when a person dies, for example.

Withdrawal from areas where the young person usually had an interest is another possible symptom. They may sleep a lot, look and act tired, and withdraw from sports or social interactions that interested them in the past.

Linked to suicide is depression. There are many reasons people get depressed. Even as adults we have experienced depression at times in our lives. It is an emotion that comes with stress, and it also can be a reaction to any form of rejection.

Ultimately, suicide is escape. As difficult as it seems to understand, the person who commits suicide is getting rid of pain, usually emotional and psychological. At the moment of the act, it is perceived as something "good" for them.

We see the opportunity of a young life to change and flourish, so we always view it as a tragedy. It is possible for a young person to talk about suicide just to get attention or to even manipulate an adult. But this is an area where you need to exercise caution. If you believe the mentee you are working with is depressed and having thoughts of suicide, inform members of the team, including the program coordinator. And during the residential phase, inform the chaplain, too.

APPLICATION TO MENTOR

It is not within your power as a mentor to totally prevent a youth from considering or committing suicide. If you have a concern, you must share it with other members of the mentoring program team. If you are a part of a faith community, you can bring hope to youth by sharing God's plan for their life. You can help them to cope with any stress at home, at school, or among peers by being positive, an empathetic listener and an encourager. As a mentor, continue to build a relationship and try to reinforce all that is good in the young person. When necessary, professional assistance may be called for. The team will make that determination.

Chapter 35

Why Some Mentors Do Not Report Suicidal Symptoms

"'I know the plans I have for you,' declares the LORD.
'They are plans for peace and not disaster, plans to give
you a future filled with hope.'"

Jeremiah 29:11

WHY SOME MENTORS DO NOT REPORT SUICIDAL SYMPTOMS

Some mentors do not report suicidal symptoms. Often a mentor is not completely sure but only has a hunch about suicidal intentions and issues they must be vigilant about.

Vague Symptoms

The reason for their hesitancy is because with suicide, as an example, rarely will a youth say "I'm going to kill myself tonight." Instead they will send out little signals. Since the mentor is an adult, they must rely on intuition and err on the conservative side. As an example, if a youth appears depressed and makes a statement like "I'm thinking of ending it all," it is better for the mentor to report the possibility of suicide rather than assume that the youth is just trying to get attention. With open discussion, you can ask the youth for elaboration.

Abuse is another example of an unreported symptom. Some forms of abuse can be subtle. We can see bruises on a person's face, but not on the entire body. Often it is the mood of the youth that gives cause for suspicion and concern. They may be sullen and withdrawn and refuse to talk about a specific parent or relative.

Fear of Overreaction

Sometimes mentors will not report abuse because they are afraid of being labeled as overreacting. But the program coordinator will actually commend you for being vigilant.

A mentor should never allow a youth to make them promise not to tell a parent or authority figure about anything they suspect. It is your responsibility as a mentor to report anyone you think has injured or may injure the youth you are working with. It is better to act in the best interest of a child and to protect them, than to fear consequences of misjudgment that may be mostly imaginary.

APPLICATION TO MENTOR

Sometimes mentors fail to report signs of depression, possible suicide and physical or sexual abuse because they fear an overreaction or making a wrong guess. One of the reasons you have been chosen to be a mentor in this program is because of your life experience and common sense. Trust your instincts. Even if you are wrong, no harm is done. The greater harm is in not passing the information and having the youth seriously hurt or harmed. When in doubt, discuss any concerns with your program coordinator.

Chapter 36

Helping Youth Manager Anger

"Love cures people - both the ones who give it
and the ones who receive it."

Karl Menninger

HELPING YOUTH MANAGE ANGER

Go into almost any juvenile facility in America and ask institutionalized youth if they have a problem with anger and you will get a 90% response or more. Texas has one of the best programs in the country that deal with anger management with delinquents.

Everyone Gets Angry

As adults we know there is justifiable anger, we call it *righteous indignation.* But this only happens on occasion. As a mentor, you recognize you get angry when you get cut off by a motorist in traffic, when a salesman sells us a defective product or makes a false claim, or someone intentionally tries to hurt us or gossip about us. There is not a person on the face of this planet that does not get angry, but being an adult means that we have learned to control it. Those in the faith community have also learned the power of forgiveness, reconciliation and the restoration of relationships.

Forgiveness

As a mentor you will find the youth may think of forgiveness as a foreign concept, if not one that makes no sense. Youth involved in gangs have found retaliation a normal response for their subculture. Getting back at a perceived enemy seems natural for some youth.

One of the benefits of a mentor relationship is the ability to introduce such foreign concepts into the life of a young person. They can literally be liberated by the discovery, freedom and power it gives an individual when they let go of anger and practice forgiveness.

Reconciliation

Reconciliation takes two parties, of course. As a mentor you may have the opportunity to bring together a parent and child and let each listen and then say words of healing. Forgiveness is a vital experience that will help the young person for the duration of their life.

Rage

Anger becomes self destructive when it is left unharnessed. When it becomes rage, it is more than a mere temper tantrum. Some of the crimes the incarcerated youth committed may have involved the uncontrolled anger and rage that they were feeling that became a negative, criminal behavior.

Diffusing Anger

Rather than denying that you have ever experienced anger, you are in a unique position as a mentor to teach them how you learned to control it. In your own life you may have practiced simply walking away from a situation that would fuel your anger, breathing deeply, counting to ten, or simply thinking good thoughts and regaining your composure.

Keep in mind that sometimes the anger that a youth feels is understandable. They may have been neglected, abandoned or a victim of physical or sexual abuse. The source of the anger may be legitimate, so be a good listener.

Some youth have learned the behavior of uncontrolled anger by watching it modeled in their home. Others have experienced injustice or become angry as a defense reaction to a fear or threat. Sometimes when a youth's anger is very deep seated they may need the services of a professional counselor. Your team may advise you about a case plan to help the youth, if this is the case.

APPLICATION TO MENTOR

To understand a youth's anger you must listen for the deeper and major problem. Anger is often a defense against pain. This can be the pain of low self-esteem, feeling isolated from others and rejected. Sometimes anger and sadness are closely linked. Most anger comes from frustration. Both are emotions, but aggression, the physical acting out, is sometimes aimed at hurting a person or sometimes destroying property. The mentor is in a position to help understand the root causes of a youth's anger by looking at the whole situation. As a mentor, you do not have to feel you must solve every problem. More of the changes in life at an adolescent age create some of the tension and anxiety that is observed in frustration and anger. A mentor can teach a young person a coping mechanism, which most adults have learned in order to handle the small annoyances that we experience every day in living life. As a mentor, you should always remain in control and calm. Even if angrily challenged by the teen, there is no need for an immediate response. You can pause, wait and form an appropriate verbal response. When a young person is looking for a fight verbally, you do not have to respond. Let them "vent," so to say. Remember, poor self-image or self-concept is often behind the mask of anger. Your affirmation will help youth manager anger.

Warning Signs of Youth Violence

"I'm convinced that nine out of every ten persons
seeing a psychiatrist do not need one.
They need somebody who will love them."

Paul Tournier

WARNING SIGNS OF YOUTH VIOLENCE

There are times in the relationship when you will help the youth with strong emotions of anger. As a mentor, if you have any question as to whether the youth has the capability of violence against you, others or in a school setting, you should consult your program coordinator.

Here are some warning signs:

1. If you observe the youth hitting or kicking walls or doors or they tell you they have recently.

2. The youth may have had a history of violent or aggressive behavior related to you by the program coordinator.

3. If you observe a youth's notebook that has violent drawings, notes or writings.

4. If the youth is increasingly withdrawn from peers and social activities.

5. If the youth tells you they feel persecuted or picked on by peers.

APPLICATION TO MENTOR

If a parent tells you that their child is spending excessive time in their room or spending time with peers that are questionable, you can make that a matter of conversation. If you sense the youth is potentially dangerous, because of violent outbursts or destructive behaviors, do not keep it to yourself. Always keep communication open, listen to the youth's reason for anger and frustrations without having to respond, defend or lecture. Do not over react if some or many of these warning signs appear. Share it with the program coordinator and probation officer and allow them to develop a plan.

Chapter 38

A Youth's Fear of Failure

"When you know that God loves you,

it helps you love yourself.

And when you love yourself,

you can love somebody else."

Kari Milton

A YOUTH'S FEAR OF FAILURE

Occasionally youth who have been institutionalized become accustomed to the structure, the uniform dress code, the supplied meals, counseling and predictable routine. For some, their life is safer and even "better" within an institution. Of course, being in a facility is not the long-term plan. Eventually they need to return home and their community.

But a few, some in long-term residential care, may have a fear of "success" and even set themselves up for failure. How do they do this? Most obvious is any return to criminal activity. This can be through the use of drugs or anti-social gang behaviors, as well as more overt crimes.

The high-risk youth in a program have not always experienced achievement in traditional ways. These are not usually youth who wear a school jacket with a letter, who have performed a piano recital or have scored the winning touchdown in a football game.

Fringe

Because, in many ways, the youth you will develop a relationship with have lived on the fringe of their community and schools, they may have a natural fear that they will fail at anything they attempt; a job, school, or better relationships at home. This perception is partly based on a history of past failures.

Identify Factors

The best way for a mentor to address these fears is to talk about them. As the youth begins to identify the factors that create anxiety, it is better to mutually come up with a set of goals that can be measured in short time increments such as weekly.

APPLICATION TO MENTOR

As a mentor your affirmation and encouragement in even the smallest achievements will help create a growing, healthy self-esteem. If the goals are too great or grandiose, youth can easily become frustrated. Try to keep the goals small and measurable and encourage the young person along the way. That is the best way to defeat any fear of success or failure.

Chapter 39

Mentor/Mentee Money Issues

"Life is a series of relapses and recoveries "

George Ade

MENTOR/MENTEE MONEY ISSUES

At some point, post-residential, a youth may ask for financial help. This is one factor that has to be dealt with in a straightforward manner with him or her.

A mentor is not an ATM machine. You are not to give the youth money on request and never on demand. The only possible exception is if the youth is mowing your lawn and you are compensating them for that job. It would be fair to pay them what you would pay any other youth to mow your lawn, and certainly not to accept service for free, for the sake of appearing to use the youth.

Work Ethic

When it comes to the subject of money, an important role of the mentor is to teach youth responsibility. Part of that education is developing a strong work ethic, helping them get a job, and learning how to manage their money correctly. This is difficult in some environments when youth see drug dealers and criminals making thousands of dollars a week when their job pays them minimum wage. But resisting anti-social activity is part of building the character of the youth you are working with.

You must help the youth to grow past a desire for instant gratification and wanting money for material possessions to responsibly use funds that they will earn through hard work.

Charitable Giving

A mentor also has a great opportunity to teach youth about giving. They can give a portion of their money for a church collection or to a charity or even donate money to causes such as a local shelter or the Salvation Army helping less fortunate people.

Withhold Credit Cards

By no means should a mentor ever give a youth their credit card. It is simply a temptation too great. Most teenagers would not be able to handle it properly. Professionals know from experience that many adults have problems in this area, as the average amount of credit card debt in America is several thousand dollars per person.

It is perfectly acceptable to take a youth to a fast food restaurant and pay for the meal. It would also be acceptable to pay for moderate price tickets to a sporting event or the cinema.

Good Breaks

At times a youth may make a request not for cash but for a material possession. In the beginning, a card and encouraging note is far more acceptable than a cash or material gift for a birthday. Giving a youth a book at Christmas would be far more acceptable than a gift such as a video game or play station.

In developing the character of the youth, you may refer to classic books such as *Pilgrim's Progress, Treasure Island, Little Women, A Christmas Carol, Anne of Green Gables, Seawolf, Tom Sawyer, Oliver Twist* and *Moby Dick,* and buy them a copy with an encouraging inscription.

Assistance Through the State

Likewise, avoid financial handouts to family members. You may have a single mom who is struggling, but the mentor should not become involved in trying to support the youth's parent. You can be a resource in the community for a single mom struggling to receive assistance. There are many programs that provide food assistance and other help throughout the state or locally.

Set Limitations

This general principle of not giving excessive handouts also applies to services. Occasionally giving youth a ride to a school event is acceptable. A mentor is not to become a taxi, however. Youth have got to find ways to share rides with other peers. You should not be at their call. The mentor can actually harm the relationship by allowing themselves to be manipulated.

In conclusion, keep cash and money or materials with monetary value like a roll of stamps out of the relationship. You may be tempting a youth to use the money to buy drugs or another illegal behavior. Modest expenditures are acceptable, of course.

APPLICATION TO MENTOR

Mentors can teach valuable lessons about being responsible with money, saving, avoiding overuse of credit and comparing price values. The mentor is not "Santa Claus" and must be vigilant about trying to win over the youth through large purchases or succumbing to a youth's request for money or high priced items.

Chapter 40

Youth's Perception of Time

"You must have long range goals to keep you from being frustrated by short range failures."

Charles Noble

YOUTH'S PERCEPTION OF TIME

We assume that the mentor and the mentee live in the same world, which they do. They are obviously on the same time zone, or they would never have a meeting.

We do not use time in this chapter to mean what our wristwatch or clocks tell us, but rather the sense of time that youth have. A Harvard professor, Dr. Edward Banfield, has written about the time perception of youth subcultures.

He says this, "the more real the future is to people, the more they will be willing to make present sacrifices to enjoy future rewards." As an example, youth will finish school and even attend a community college or a university because he is able to see the long-term benefits of the sacrifices he is making in the present toward a good education. According to his research, youth who fail in school do not always have a lack of ability, they simply do not have a clear picture of who they can become in the future.

A part of adolescent developmental psychology is the need for instant gratification seeking pleasure such as "getting high" with peers without considering long-term consequences.

According to Dr. Banfield, "Some youth cannot give up pleasures of the present for some deferred gratification in the future they cannot even conceptualize."

As a mentor, you have made many sacrifices in life that had long-term goals. You completed an education. Many of you were married and raised children. You have had career advancement that was progressive.

The mentor can help the youth to see a future that is real and begin to take steps to prepare for it.

A sociologist, Dr. Anthony Campolo, says it this way, "For a significant portion of American teenagers, time perception is becoming increasingly confined to the present."

Helping youth develop a vocational plan is one way to teach them about present day sacrifices for a long-term goal. This present age of natural disasters where hundreds if not thousands are swept away by tsunami waves, buried beneath debris by an earthquake or hurricane and the random senselessness of terrorist acts contribute to youth being pessimistic about the world they live in and concentrating on short term goals.

Living for instant rewards can have an effect on the spirituality of youth as well. They may seek instant "signs" of their beliefs. They want healing, God's blessing or a response to prayer immediately.

There are some concepts that are foreign to youth but familiar to mentors. Words like *sacrifice* mean that we can put aside our own needs for gratification in service to others.

APPLICATION TO MENTOR

Moving youth toward seeing a future that is real and goals that are achievable are important goals. The youth you are working with cannot imagine themselves as an adult, as a husband, wife or father. It would be more difficult for them to make good choices such as completing their education when they cannot envision how this will help them in the future.

You must work with the youth's goals a little at a time, week by week. Those who have been accustomed to only thinking in the here-and-now will not immediately make that transformation to long-term goals, but through your modeling as a mentor, you can show them the benefit of the goals you have achieved in your own lifetime.

Chapter 41

Building a Youth's Self-Esteem

"The deepest principle in human nature
is the craving to be appreciated."

William James

BUILDING A YOUTH'S SELF-ESTEEM

One of the important areas of the mentor/mentee relationship is helping the youth form a positive self-image.

This is a time in their life when how they view themselves is often a challenge. They compare themselves to other teens and even "good" teens not in the justice system. Something that may not be of major concern to an adult can become a major issue. A youth may be concerned that he or she is fat, has acne, or is awkward in sports.

Youth Issues

Adults from time-to-time will worry about bills, income tax deadlines, and major home repairs, while youth are mostly concerned about fitting in with their peers. That is why they spend so much time in front of a mirror. The girls, as well as the boys, are concerned about their hair and what they wear. An event like failing to pass a driver's test can be monumental to the self-image of a teen.

Develop Youth Skills

Many young people have a fear of failure. Not everyone was designed to be a great football player, of course. The mentor is in a unique position to help encourage the youth in areas where they have special skills or abilities. For some it is music and drama, for others it is expressing themselves in writing and poetry. Every child has a gift, and the mentor can encourage and affirm the young person, which will affect their self-esteem.

Spiritual Positives

In the church community, it is important to balance the concept of sin or wrong behavior with self-esteem. Sometimes a young person will assume that they are not worthy of God's attention and dwell on their poor behavior rather than the self-worth that can also be found in the sacred writings of every major religion.

APPLICATION TO MENTOR

As you talk and listen to the youth, do not accept self-deprecating phrases like "I'm such a klutz," "I'm stupid," or "I can't do anything right." The youth you work with should not be compared to anyone else. They need to develop self-worth as an individual. Take time in the relationship to affirm, to encourage and to help the young person accept themselves, just as you have accepted them unconditionally.

Mentoring Boundaries

"He who sows courtesy reaps friendship,
and he who plants kindness gathers love."

St. Basil

MENTORING BOUNDARIES

There are some necessary and obvious boundaries in mentoring. Acting as a professional psychologist, certified counselor or social worker is not acceptable. As a mentor, you may have an advanced degree and even be a social worker, but the relationship with the youth should never be treated as a case or as a client. Juvenile justice systems have professionals in the residential phase who are competent. The mentor must always maintain the role as a link for the youth between the residential and the community and family.

Keeping Neutral

While a mentor will naturally bond with the youth, they must be careful not to try to replace any family members. It is more important for the mentor to try to strengthen those existing parental relationships, not to agree with youth who criticize parents, but to lead them to understanding.

Encouraging Forgiveness

It is predictable for a boy to see a father figure in an adult man, especially when his own father is missing. At some point the father may reenter his life or the youth may have the ability to forgive any of the father's neglect or abuse. This is a preferred strategy.

No Competition

The mentor should be watchful of any potential rivalry where the parent, often a single mom, feels threatened by the mentor/mentee relationship. This can best be approached by adequate communication where the mentor informs the parent of their goals and wherever possible tries to bring the youth and the parent together when reconciliation is necessary.

Never Criticize a Facility

During the residential phase, the mentor should never side with the youth against any facility or administrative policies. These policies are in place and in practice for good reason. Youth will naturally rebel against constraints. A mentor may not even agree with how a facility or a program is run, but it is very important for them to keep neutral, keep such opinions to themselves, and to make no leading statements that would criticize the residential phase.

Recruit Tutors

A mentor is not a tutor, although it is possible you can assist the youth in certain subject areas. It is far better to identify other adults in a church or in a community who can tutor in certain subjects and keep the mentoring relationship in the area of advisor, coach and friend.

Know Limitations

A mentor is never the "Shell Answer-Man," that is to say that you will not have the answers to all of a youth's problems or questions, nor should you be expected to. That is why a team is in place and you can seek guidance from the program coordinator. Also a support network of other mentors can help when a situation arises that is foreign to the mentor.

Patience

A mentor should certainly not expect a quick and dramatic change in a youth. It took many years for a youth to develop bad patterns and bad decision making, and those temptations and negative influences will still be present in the community. It is better to take it step-by-step and day-by-day and congratulate the youth in all the small victories.

Trust is Earned

Confidentiality and trust are essential for a mentoring relationship. You should always keep the subjects discussed confidential unless you inform the youth by law or by policy that there is certain information you must pass on. As an example, if you suspect the youth is being abused physically, sexually or emotionally, you are obligated to tell the program coordinator and not keep it to yourself. You must also inform the youth that you will be passing this information on. The same is true for depression or the possibility of suicide. For the best interest of the youth, this information should not be kept to the mentor.

If the youth tells about criminal behavior or illegal drug use, you are bound to pass that information on.

Set Limits

A mentor is not the servant of the youth. You are not at their call. A request must be reasonable. You are not obligated to spend large sums of money on athletic events or entertainment or become their taxi service. Appropriately setting boundaries and saying "no" is a better teaching example than complying with every request.

As a mentor, you must remain an adult and the youth stays a youth. The goals of the relationship is not for the youth to become a copy of you in dress, talk or behavior. You may share an interest in music and movies but it is unlikely that you will play the same video games or attend a rock concert together. With discretion, you may participate in some of these activities but more as a sounding board for proper choices, as a guidepost in the wilderness of the youth's culture.

It is never appropriate to share your personal problems or burdens with the youth. It is far better to use an example of a problem that you overcame in your past and how you solved the problem. The youth is never there to meet your emotional needs. Co-dependency would be a very poor pattern in the mentor/mentee relationship.

Stay an Adult

You are the adult and the two of you are never "'buddies". You are there because you have life experiences and in most cases the stability of many years of marriage, raising children, going to college, paying taxes, going to work, voting, serving on jury duty, belonging to a church or a fraternal organization. What you may consider your normal life, your day-in and day-out living, is what is most valuable for your mentee. Like most of us you have made some poor decisions in life, but you have also made far more good decisions. While you may not think as the youth does, you can help adapt your wisdom and life experiences to their situation whenever possible.

APPLICATION FOR MENTOR

Boundaries keep the relationship adult to youth. As a mentor, you will have an opportunity to impact the youth's life in multiple areas such as education, social skills and even health. By having boundaries, you are encouraged to bring in other resources, use members of the team and other community services. One important boundary is to not replace a parent or to play the role of social worker or therapist. While you can facilitate communication between the parent and child, having a caring, positive relationship with the youth is your main goal as a mentor. Youth are most helped by a positive relationship that builds on trust and empathy. Case management and therapy are organized by other members of the team. Your goal is to develop a relationship that affirms and encourages them to make good decisions.

Chapter 43

When Mentors Get
Out of Bounds

"Be what you would have your pupils to be."

Thomas Carlyle

WHEN MENTORS GET OUT OF BOUNDS

Supervision and ongoing training are the best factors to keep mentors within both program boundaries and personal boundaries.

Sometimes a mentor may even try to meet some of their own emotional needs through a relationship, and it is important for the program coordinator to identify that and make adjustments as soon as possible. Here are some examples:

1. **Limitations** - A mentor should not try to meet their personal emotional needs through the youth they mentor. Sometimes during the course of a relationship, they may become separated from a spouse, go through a painful divorce, have financial difficulties, including a bankruptcy, and these are not subjects they need to burden the youth with. The primary focus is on the youth's behaviors and goals and never their own.

2. **Boundaries** - A mentor is not a "pal" or a "buddy" to the youth they mentor. There must be strong generational boundaries. They remain an adult and the youth remains a minor. This does not mean they would not necessarily go to a ballgame or a rock concert together. Mentoring activities are about guidance, not hanging out together.

3. **Family** - The mentor is not really part of the family or part of family gatherings or social events. It may be very natural for a single mom to invite the mentor to come to a picnic, but this should be avoided until after many months in the relationship. The mentor is not replacing parents, and as such should never try to fill that role. Obviously a mentor has to avoid any family friendships that could become a romantic entanglement with a single mom or a single dad.

4. **Stay with major problems** - The mentor is available as a resource when the youth is having major problems. Every person in life has minor problems and it is not a goal of the mentor to deal with every single problem or to be on call. Above all, the mentor is not the child's psychotherapist. Mentoring works best when there is a healthy relationship and

204

there are clear limitations, sometimes even written in the form of a contract.

5. **Having empathy** - It is important for a mentor to know the difference between empathy and sympathy. As an example, you can say that you care about a situation without getting emotional or even crying. The child really does not need sympathy, they need a strong person who can maintain control and simply empathize with their problems.

6. **Don't give up** - There will be times when you will see setbacks in a young person's life. A girl may get pregnant or a boy father a child, as examples. Do not give up and do not be disappointed. When someone has been in the juvenile justice system and has had considerable emotional baggage, it can be a process of two steps forward and one step back. Be patient. Be kind. And do not give up the first time there is a setback.

APPLICATION TO MENTOR

The warning signs of an ineffective mentor are best seen by a program coordinator or a mentor supervisor and are transgressing personal and generational boundaries. As an example, taking setbacks personally, trying to "save" the child, giving up when there is a setback or even becoming a family member or replacing parents. Perhaps as a mentor you are experiencing "burn out." You may require a *time out* and meet with a personal mentor. Often a mentor who transgresses boundaries needs additional training.

The Ten Commandments Of
Mentor Relationships

"Immediate payment for service may not be great
but the retirement plan is out of this world."

Anonymous

THE TEN COMMANDMENTS OF MENTOR RELATIONSHIPS

The Ten Commandments are universally respected by Jews and Christians. They have been adapted here (with some levity) to explain the important factors of developing a relationship.

1. THOU SHALT PLACE NO OTHER ACTIVITIES AHEAD OF YOUR PROMISES TO A YOUTH.

2. THOU SHALT MEMORIZE THE NAMES OF THE YOUTH AND HIS FAMILY.

3. REMEMBER THE DAY OF YOUR MEETING AND ALWAYS SHOW UP ON TIME.

4. RESPECT THE MOTHER AND FATHER OF THE YOUTH (or guardian).

5. NEVER MURDER YOUR RELATIONSHIP WITH THE YOUTH BY BEING PREACHY OR JUDGEMENTAL.

6. NEVER TRY TO BE A SUBSTITUTE PARENT, PEER OR BUDDY, JUST BE YOURSELF.

7. NEVER STEAL A YOUTH'S DESIRE TO SHARE WITH YOU BY SPEAKING TOO MUCH.

8. NEVER LIE OR PRETEND TO UNDERSTAND THEIR MUSIC, CULTURE OR HEROES IF YOU DON'T.

9. NEVER DESIRE TO BE ANYTHING OTHER THAN REAL AND HONEST WITH THE YOUTH.

10. ENCOURAGE EVERYONE AT ALL TIMES. ENCOURAGE THE YOUTH, HIS OR HER FAMILY, OTHER MENTORS AND STAFF.

Chapter 45

The Ultimate Role Model

"God does not love us because we are valuable.
We are valuable because God loves us."

Fulton Sheen

THE ULTIMATE ROLE MODEL

His name is Jesus. He is probably the ultimate role model

He was a historical figure, a real human being, who literally changed and influenced the world. He never wrote a book, yet more books have been written about him than any other person in history.

He never went to a university, but his teachings are widely used. The very calendar the world uses is based upon the time of his birth.

Jesus may be the ultimate role model. Why? Even the Greeks during the years following the death of Jesus began to embrace his teachings. That is because the Greek civilization always placed a high value on those who gave and lived good examples.

Consider some of the attributes that we know from those who walked with him, who were his disciples, in mentoring terminology his "mentees."

- As a child he respected his parents and cared for his mother long after the death of his father.

- He was kind to everyone except those who mislead and manipulated people in the name of religion.

- He did not distinguish between classes but was equally comfortable with rich and poor people.

- He was patient with one of his disciples, Peter, even when Peter was emotional, temperamental and boastful. He tolerated the criticism of Judas, a man who would eventually betray Jesus.

- Jesus was not arrogant or pretentious, but instead humble.

- Even standing before those who falsely accused him, he did not repay evil for evil but at the end of his earthly life forgave his enemies.

Some will say he is a perfect person. We all know that perfection is not attainable. But nonetheless his actions and his personality make him an excellent role model.

All major religions respect him and his teachings apart from any theological teachings or beliefs.

APPLICATION TO MENTOR

If you belong to a Christian church it will be easy to share the actions and words of Jesus with your mentee because you know him as Savior and Lord. If you are Jewish or Muslim, your religion may respect him as a wise teacher. There is nothing about his life that is not worth modeling, and many of his stories (parables) are easily applied to youth including *The Good Samaritan* and *The Prodigal Son.*

Chapter 46

The Importance of Forgiveness

"Be kind and compassionate to one another,

forgiving each other,

just as in Christ God forgave you."

Ephesians 4:32

THE IMPORTANCE OF FORGIVENESS

There is probably nothing more important as a young person grows in their Christian faith than to understand the role of forgiveness.

Many of the youth who have been in the juvenile justice system have emotional wounds. Neglectful parents or guardians have sometimes hurt them. They may have been physically or sexually abused. They may have experienced rejection from the school or even the court system, and whether real or perceived, there is only one appropriate response for a Christian and that is to forgive.

Most youth who have belonged to juvenile gangs find this concept totally foreign. The rule of the street is retaliation. When someone hurts us, we hurt them. It is a street survival skill called *payback*.

Many youth will not think of this gang behavior as vengeance but simply a natural part of survival in street culture. Teaching them to forgive their enemies or those who hurt them will not happen overnight. You must direct them to the Scriptures, especially the teachings of Christ that speak of forgiveness. Jesus said to a woman caught in adultery, "Neither do I condemn you, go and sin no more," John 8:11.

Whenever possible, you should model forgiveness yourself by telling them briefly about people who have hurt you and how you have forgiven them. It is important to teach young people that forgiveness is not simply something done in words but can take place through restitution or a written or verbal apology. It is never casual. It takes effort and determination. Again, this is not easy for many young people, but it is one of the most important concepts that you can give to a young person growing in their faith.

Even adult Christians struggle with forgiveness. We sometimes have real enemies, not exaggerated or imaginary. When we have encountered a person, sometimes in our own church, who has willfully tried to hurt us, the natural instinct is to be defensive or to want to get back at someone or at least hold a grudge.

This is probably the hardest teaching of Jesus. If the Father is to forgive us, we must forgive those who have hurt us. Even more than that, we must bless our enemies. It says in Matthew 6:14, "If you forgive men when they sin against you, your heavenly Father will also forgive you."

If you listen to a young person talk long enough, you will eventually hear hurts. They will have grudges against a missing father, a probation officer, a teacher or anyone they perceive has hurt them. It does not matter whether the hurt is real or perceived. It is what a person feels that is real because that is what they act on.

In a young person, hurt often transforms into anger, and at its worse anger becomes aggression. As a mentor, you are in a position of authority to help prevent any form of acting out or aggression that can result in a crime or get them back into the juvenile justice system.

APPLICATION TO MENTOR

Faith-based mentoring must focus on key issues, and in Christianity nothing is more compelling than our command to forgive our enemies.

You may work for a whole year on this issue and may experience the youth having lapses. They may use swear words about someone they do not like, hold grudges, or they may even talk about "getting even" with that person.

Continue to listen in a non-judgmental way so that all the feelings and thoughts get out. It is only when all the bile is finally spilled that you begin to map a strategy together of how you can take the steps to forgive their enemy.

Remember, Jesus had real enemies who were out to get him. They had trumped up charges and a mock hearing. Eventually they killed him. But on the cross Jesus said, "Father, forgive them," Luke 23:24.

Do not expect forgiveness to be easy for young people. Anyone who was involved in a juvenile gang has a natural instinct for revenge and retaliation. Progress slowly but be persistent because this will be one of the earmarks of a growing faith.

Chapter 47

Sharing Christ With the Family

"I would not give much for your religion unless it can be
seen. Lamps do not talk, but they do shine."

Charles Spurgeon

SHARING CHRIST WITH THE FAMILY

Your principle responsibility as a mentor is to the youth. You want to have good communication with the family, as their support is going to be helpful whenever the youth fails to return a phone call or show up for a visit.

The way in which you share your faith with the family must be natural. That means they first of all need to see Christ in you, and if what they see in you is genuine and authentic the times for sharing will usually be in a crisis.

If the family member has been arrested and goes to jail or if someone becomes very sick, that is a time that they will naturally reach out to you and you can answer their questions with a good spiritual foundation.

Resist the attempt to sit in a family's home simply preaching or trying to "save" them. This can imply the wrong or a hidden agenda. If the family of the mentee is to come to Christ, then they will primarily do it by seeing the changes in their own son or daughter and by seeing your faith as something real and genuine.

Being with a young person for a year you will have challenges, disappointments and setbacks in their family. Whether it is a single mom, a grandmother or both parents, they will watch very closely how you react as a person of faith.

APPLICATION TO MENTOR

Your opportunities to show your faith with the mentee's family will most naturally happen when there is a crisis within that family. Prepare for those opportunities but never share in a forced way. Being available at a funeral, at a hospital, or when a family member has been arrested and has gone to jail is when your faith will be heard and will look most genuine.

Chapter 48

Finding A Church

"The 'how-to's' of a church has little moral impact on our society unless they see our righteousness."

Richard Halverson

FINDING A CHURCH

An important factor is to invite the youth to your church. This will be a group of people willing to help the youth on several levels. Some examples include; social skills (people skills), practical skills like balancing a checkbook, learning how to cook and a tutor assisting with studies. (Refer to Chapter 28, Building a Church Support Group for more information.)

I do not recommend one particular church be identified as a church where young ex-offenders attend. It is important that many churches be involved within the community and not label these young people as *ex-offenders*.

You need to be respectful if the parents practice a different faith or belong to a different denomination. If the youth is going to depart from their religious tradition or family heritage, this must be the young person's choice and never appear forced.

A parent or parents who see productive change in the young person will be supportive of any choices made if it happens over time and naturally.

Always respect the religious preferences of the young person. Some might easily enjoy a charismatic service where others prefer something more organized in terms of liturgy or even a quiet tradition. There are some churches more associated with a particular race and culture and that should be respected as well.

The more church people are involved with a young person, the more that transition is going to be smooth.

The question often becomes, Should the mentor and mentee attend the same church? That is fine, but I do not think it is necessary, since the mentor is not really a part of the family and should not appear as a step-parent. Attending a church together might send the wrong message. They can certainly assist the church-going of the young person by giving them a ride or setting up transportation.

The first concern of mentoring should not be "saving" the youth, not in the sense of an evangelistic agenda. The youth need to see Christ in you, and if they naturally ask questions like, **How can I go to heaven? Is there life after death?** then one can naturally answer those questions.

Mentoring is not necessarily a Bible study. This is a caution. There are Bible studies that young people can become involved in, and certainly as a mentor you can quote the Scriptures, but mentoring is more about developing a relationship, basically a friendship. And most friends do not talk about the Bible during every single conversation. It is okay to talk about sports, music and the fields that interest the young person.

APPLICATION TO MENTOR

If you have been a mentor for almost a year, your encouragement for the young person to attend church will be very important, but it is not necessary for the youth to attend the same church you do. Respect whatever cultural and racial preferences the mentee may have regarding a worship experience. The most important thing is not church attendance but a faith witness, a faith that is real, that is discipled and is growing in the mentor and hopefully the youth.

When the Relationship Ends

"Mentoring cannot take place outside of a relationship."

Ted Engstrom

WHEN THE RELATIONSHIP ENDS

There is a formal ending to every mentor relationship, but that does not mean the relationship ends.

As I have noted, I have personally continued to communicate with people that I mentored as long as twenty years ago, but I do not talk with them frequently or meet with them every week. Usually a mentoring relationship will last for a year after the residential phase for a juvenile and perhaps six months while they are confined to a facility.

Most worthy goals can be accomplished in that time, and most formal programs will require that as a goal. By mutual consent, both the adult and the youth can continue the mentoring relationship longer than a year, if it is a healthy relationship.

There is a natural cycle to most mentoring relationships, and you should allow that cycle to take place. Never burn bridges or leave angry. Even if you have not seen significant progress, it is okay to naturally move on to a relationship with another young person and keep limited contact with the former mentee.

Many mentors have a new mentee relationship every year, and that can be both normal and healthy. It is not advised to mentor several people at the same time. Because of the investment of time and emotional energy, that is usually not possible and not recommended.

Sometime before the year is over you can have the young person develop a relationship with a new mentor when something in the relationship and its chemistry has not worked. Do not consider that failure or rejection. It is sometimes a very natural process to have another mentor take over where there are limits to how far you can go with a young person.

APPLICATION TO MENTOR

Accept the natural cycle that a mentor/mentee relationship will end in approximately one year, and sometimes sooner if they require a new mentor. Never consider it failure or rejection if you have not achieved all of your goals as a mentor. Many times you have planted seeds that you may not realize will blossom years later. As it says in Philippians 1:6, "He who began a good work in you will carry it on to completion until the day of Christ Jesus."

Chapter 50

Measuring An Effective Mentor

"Therefore, if anyone is in Christ, he is a new creation;
the old has gone, the new has come!"

2 Corinthians 5:17

MEASURING AN EFFECTIVE MENTOR

The word *effective* is intentionally used rather than the word *good*. I do not want to engage in 'good' or 'bad' headings for a mentor but really look at the effectiveness of the relationship and whether or not we see measurable improvement in the young person.

1. **Belief** – A mentor is basically someone who believes in people and believes that they can change. A cynical mentor is probably a contradiction in terms. This is a person who invests their time and emotional energy into relationship and they must believe that the person is capable of changing. A mentor who believes the power of God can change people has the resource of the Holy Spirit.

2. **Celebrate victories** – More important is celebrating small victories. That simply means that along the way there will be moments of enlightenment where a young person may stop skipping school or work harder and progress from getting Cs to Bs, and those small victories should be celebrated. If your goals are too high and you are looking for complete change of a young person's habits or personality, as a mentor you will continually be frustrated. Take it slow.

3. **Patience** – Taking the time to get to know the young person is essential for the success of the relationship. Never try to rush or force a relationship. There are no short cuts. It takes listening and the investment of many meetings before you will even see progress. People who have emotional wounds or baggage will not open up to another person immediately. Like a flower, let the petals open slowly and by themselves and never force them.

4. **Help with needs** – The needs I refer to are *some* of their needs not all of their needs. You are not on call 24 hours a day, seven days a week. Obviously there can be an emergency call after midnight, but you need to set very clear boundaries as to what is a real emergency and what can wait till the next day. Going into a relationship believing you can help a mentee with some of their

needs is far more practical and realistic than believing you are going to meet all their needs.

5. **Be an encourager** – In the Bible one of the early disciples named Joseph actually had his name changed to Barnabas. Barnabas means *encourager*. He actually had his name changed to fit his character and to match his lifestyle. That is a wonderful example of what a mentor does in the life of a person. You encourage them to be a little more than what they might believe they are capable of. Encourage them to trust God to meet their true needs.

APPLICATION TO MENTOR

A mentor should see progress in family relationships, attendance and grades in school, politeness, and the rejection of drugs, alcohol and gang interaction. An affirmation of faith and trust in God is vital for a youth with a troubled background to accept God's mercy, develop spiritual gifts, and truly be a *new creation* through new birth in Christ.

Chapter 51

How to Screen for Mentors

"The Spirit himself testifies with our spirit

that we are God's children."

Romans 8:16

HOW TO SCREEN FOR MENTORS

1. When working with youth, a criminal background check for an adult mentor is very important. Anyone who has committed a crime against a child, especially a pedophile, has no place in a formal mentoring program. But also watch for those on the edge such as people who were arrested but not convicted of any form of child molesting or even failure to pay child support.

2. Check references. You want your mentor to be an established member of a local church and you want a strong reference from a pastor. You also want someone other than a family member who has known them for three to five years.

3. A mentor can be single but a person who is married should have a healthy and stable relationship and have control of their own family and children as it says in the Scriptures.

4. A mentor needs to be a person who can make commitments and keep them. Mentoring involves a lot of time. And if a potential mentor is a very busy individual who travels frequently, be sure that this is a commitment they can keep.

5. A mentor needs to be humble and trainable. Someone who comes into a program having all the answers may not be attentive in a training situation. They must also utilize the support network and the support system of other mentors so they will be able to learn from any mistakes they make.

6. Pairing transcends age or race, so those factors are not important. A 75-year-old black woman can be the mentor of a young girl or even a young boy. But generally keep it within the same gender. A young man in college and a young girl who is 19 is never a good match. As an overriding principle, mentor relationships should be of the same gender. Someone who insists that they have to be with someone of the opposite sex may be sending up a red flag.

7. Effective mentors are people that can maintain generational boundaries and personal boundaries. They should not be having the youth sleep over in their home or going on unsupervised camping trips without other adults present. Remember, even though someone has not been convicted as a pedophile, supervision is the best way to keep any potential harm from happening.

8. Good mentors are good listeners. People who feel they are called to preach to children or give continual advice will actually shut down the relationship, even if the youth is polite enough to smile and nod their head. Make sure you cultivate mentors who really understand that listening is both an art and a skill.

9. The religious convictions of mentors in a faith-based program should be orthodox and agree with the basic church creeds. A program may want to develop a faith statement that is general but not too distinctive. If, for instance, you insist on having people who speak in tongues, your program will become a group of charismatic mentors, which is not a healthy or holistic program. A Roman Catholic who believes that Jesus is the way to salvation and not through the Vatican or the Pope can certainly be a mentor. And a Baptist who gets too hung up on denominational rules may not be as effective. Christians come in all shapes and sizes but the core belief that faith in Jesus is essential for salvation must be consistent.

10. Can a mentor be an ex-offender? Absolutely. Someone who has been in trouble when they were a youth or were even locked up in the system can be very effective, even someone who was formerly in a juvenile gang. But do not make the mistake of thinking that only people who were in the system themselves can be the best or only mentors. That is like thinking that heart surgeons have to have a heart attack to really empathize with their patients. When it happens naturally, ex-offenders can be fine mentors.

11. Be sure in the training to make sure mentors do not engage in preaching. Most young people, especially in institutions, have already had a steady diet of people who come in and talk about

the perils of damnation and of going to hell. What young people need is positive encouragement and the belief that their sins are forgiven and they can start on a new path through repentance.

12. Can someone who has mentored an adult, mentor a juvenile? Yes, they can. The mentoring principles are nearly identical. It is just that it usually requires a little more patience when working with young people because youth still lack impulse control and are not easily frightened by consequences. But someone who cares about people can serve adults or youth, and those concepts are easily transferable.

13. Can a mentor be a person who does not want to work with an organized program? Initially, it is good to have supervision. Of course, someone can mentor someone outside of a traditional program but the benefits far outweigh that of the individual. Anyone can read this book and obtain good principles, but having program coordinators they can interact with and a support group of other mentors is preferable.

WHEN TO REJECT A MENTOR

Perhaps rejection is too strong a word but we can certainly screen out or give people a time-out when they are overly critical or point out all the mistakes of the young person they work with. Also, someone who is too easily manipulated or tricked by the mentee has to be watched closely.

Mentors are not perfect people but they are stable people. Program coordinators who screen need to not only pray over candidates but let more than one person be present at an interview so that they can study and discuss the person's answers later.

When having mentors fill out forms, keep in mind that self-reporting is also self-interest. Someone is always going to fill out a form to make themselves look good. It is in the actual one-on-one interview, which ought to last at least 90 minutes or longer, that you allow them to talk and take good notes.

Young people in trouble have placed limits on themselves. They have accepted into their head and into their heart messages of defeat and low self-esteem. The best mentors have experienced that in their own lives and have overcome negative self-thinking through faith and the support system of other Christians and even a personal mentor.

Finally, when selecting a mentor, they need to really like young people. Caring is not enough. We can care about the fact that a young person comes to Christ but not prefer to be with young people. They will say things that are at times silly or politically incorrect. We are the adults, they are the minors, we need to be patient.

I have always enjoyed being with young people and I believe that is a gift of the Holy Spirit. When you are called to something, you are not called to work with a population of people you cannot stand or dislike. That would be a total mismatch. Some people are called to be mentors of adults, some are called to be mentors of juveniles and some can be mentors to both populations.

When you select a mentor, make sure they truly like young people because the benefits and rewards are going to be reciprocal.

Summary

"Those who believe in a better tomorrow
become survivors."

Victor Frankl

SUMMARY

No one really makes it alone. Even though we live in a culture that talks about the "self-made man," in truth if you look at any man or woman who is successful you will find people that helped them. They are often coaches, teachers, even parents. Youth need models and heroes that are worth looking up to. And that is basically what a mentor is all about.

As Shawn Barnard, a Dallas area pastor said, "It is not all about us. It is all about God, our provider. It is not *my space* but *His space.*

When a mentor is also a disciple of Jesus and is growing in their own faith, the odds of helping the youth to stability increase because of the faith element. When we serve others we discover our true potential and value.

As it has been demonstrated in this book, never force faith but let it happen naturally. It is not so much *show and tell* but heavily weighted toward *show.* In fact, it does not really matter what you tell the youth or how much you give advice or preach, if they do not see Jesus in you. If they do not see a genuine growing faith, leading them to Christ will be nearly impossible.

Never complete a session, even if you meet weekly, without a word of encouragement.

I once worked for someone who at the end of a meeting would pull out a small little note and tell me something I had done wrong. It might have been not returning a phone call or missing the deadline of a report, but I always walked back to my office with my shoulders slumped because he ended on a negative note. He was a good man, although he was lacking in management skills. He thought it was important to keep me, as a young leader, humble. And so, pointing out my mistakes was, in his estimation, a way of discipling me.

In reality, I knew my own mistakes quite well, and because he always saved the negative messages to the end, I got the feeling that I could never be good enough, I could never, no matter how hard I worked, ever get his full approval. I do not think he meant to do this, but he actually became more like my father who hardly ever said a kind word to me or encouraged me.

I believe that every single session with a mentee should end with a word of encouragement. It is important to keep that encouragement honest. You might be thinking "why would I ever be dishonest?" The truth is that sometimes people are dishonest even in the church and they do not realize it. As an example, there are people in a church who will tell someone they can become a great rock star, win on American Idol or be an opera star when in fact they cannot sing on pitch. That is what I mean by dishonesty. Everyone has a gift, and many strive in an area where they are not gifted. Honesty and objectivity are very important. Is every child going to become President of the United States? Of course not. But they can be the mayor of their own town or serve on a board or become a deacon in their church someday. Realistic goals are more honest.

Remember as a mentor that each young generation is different from the generation earlier, so we as a mentor have to learn on a curve. We do not naturally understand their communication styles using chat rooms and blogs, but we can learn by listening. They will teach us about their techno world and culture.

As you assist the mentee's spiritual journey, helping them to write in a journal can be very effective. Let them express themselves and talk to God through a journal. This is a very personal document and they should only be encouraged to share it with you when they feel totally comfortable.

The secret to success in life is really just hard work. Few people are really a genius. Even Michelangelo, the great sculptor who had done great artworks such as the David, once said, "If you could see how hard I work, you would not call it genius."

Always be humble in your relationship with the youth. You are not there to be an idol or look like a saint. Never try to impress them with your knowledge or skills. And do not try to go too fast or take a young person where they are not willing or cannot go. We have all heard of stage moms and baseball dads who live through their children by pressuring them into sports or drama or other vocations where the child may not have a skill or an interest. Do not try to take the youth where they do not want to go.

Great coaching can only really develop someone's potential. You cannot make someone a genius in math or a star quarterback if they do not have a natural skill or a strong desire.

In the area of faith, the mentor and the mentee must share a vision; looking at life with optimism instead of fatalism, hope versus doom. The young person may not embrace Jesus Christ in the first weeks or months of the relationship, or even after a full year, but you may have simply planted seeds. But that is okay. Someone else may come along in their life; pull out the weeds and water the soil. What is important is that when they make that commitment to Christ, it be real and authentic.

Finally, all youth can improve, all can get better. They do not have to be perfect and perfection is never the goal of mentoring. If you set expectations too high, you will both be frustrated. Set them too low, and you will never know the full potential of the young person you work with.

Above all, make prayer your greatest resource. Pray every day by name for the young person you mentor. If that person comes to trust the Lord, then take time during the meeting to pray together, but never do it in a way that would embarrass the young person in a public restaurant or at a mall.

Remember the model that Jesus gave us when he called the twelve disciples; he was essentially mentoring them. Not all of us are capable of mentoring twelve people at one time, and some clearly had emotional problems, setbacks and one even betrayed Him. When we pour our life into another person's life, we not only pass on the gifts and the benefits that we have been given, but we are making this world a better place, even after we are gone.

As it said in a previous chapter, our greatest legacy is not having our name on a building or even on the cover of a book but how we have poured ourselves into the life of another person and hopefully when those changes are real, they will someday become a mentor themselves.

SUPPLEMENTAL INFORMATION
&
TRAINING ROLE PLAYS

MENTOR'S MANUAL SUPPLEMENTAL INFORMATION FOR TRAINERS

As you review this book you will find repetition of certain themes. This is intentional. The words *affirm* and *encourage* as well as the word *listen* are repeated throughout the manual. It is a redundancy put there for the sake of reinforcement.

The first few chapters define mentoring. You may wish to add in the appendix a flow chart for your facility or program that will correspond with Chapter Seven, which talks about the *Responsibilities to the Program Coordinator.*

Both *Frequently Asked Questions,* Chapter Eight, and *Mentoring Guidelines,* Chapter Nine, were put near the front of this book so that it is actually a part of the curriculum and can be referred to frequently.

Chapters 10 and 11 encourage church communities and also talk about logical boundaries.

Chapters 12 through 15 give the mentor a background. For those who have never worked with an at-risk juvenile this will give important information. The intention here was to simplify and not create something that was overly academic.

Chapters 16 and 17 specifically refer to the residential period and have suggested activities as well as safeguards.

Chapters 18 and thereafter are all practical guidelines that address issues from culture to building self-esteem and working with the family.

Take particular notice of Chapter 27, *Strengthening a Youth's Sense of Community.* In that chapter you will find some practical activities for service that the mentor and the mentee can engage in together.

Near the end of the book, Chapter 44 is a rewrite of The Ten Commandments, which are a practical guide for the youth and the mentor.

And Chapter 45 presents Jesus as the ultimate role model. In a government program you may present him as a historical figure who is respected by all major religions. In this way no one should feel a theological statement is being made. It will also not give offense to an agnostic or someone of a non Christian faith. It focuses on those parts of his behavior that were kind, non-judgmental and forgiving. However those who have faith in Jesus as Lord and Savior will understand.

The final chapters 45 through 51 incorporate clear Christian principles.

Within the Appendix is a bibliography and also a Contact Sheet that can be useful for the mentor and some supplemental material, including an interview with Dwight Harris, a known leader in juvenile justice.

Following, you will find recommendations for role-plays. Most of you are familiar with role-plays and know they can be a very effective training tool. The suggestion is to have the more difficult part, which is usually the youth especially if there is manipulation and resistance, played by the trainer. By having the mentor play himself or herself they really do not have to exaggerate or pretend to be something other than themselves.

Each of the role-plays is designed to bring out an important area that also corresponds with the manual.

TRAINING ROLE-PLAYS

The program coordinator plays an important role in teaching through example and exercises.

Role-play can be fun, humorous and a great way of having mentors observe common situations. Remember that not every adult enjoys role-play and may even be embarrassed by acting in front of a group of peers. Always make the role play voluntary and in some cases, talk to prospective volunteers ahead of time.

For the role-plays to be most effective, almost always have the mentor play himself or herself or at least play the role of a mentor. Since you know the application that you are teaching, it is best for you as the trainer or facilitator to play the role of the parent or teacher. The best role-plays exhibit a problem and you are in a better position to play, as an example, a resistant youth than would be the mentor. Do not drag out the role-play. Most role-plays can be done in three to five minutes and once the point is made, terminate the role-play then follow it with active discussion that elicits ideas from the mentors on how they could change or do something differently. Also be sure to reward and compliment the mentor for their activity. Never embarrass and certainly never humiliate someone in a role-play situation.

Here are examples of role-plays that will help the mentor visualize solutions to common problems:

1. **Personal questions**. In this role-play the trainer plays a youth who begins to ask questions that are too personal and intrusive. As an example, playing the role of a youth, he may ask the mentor about their first sexual experience and ask for details such as location and age. Or you may ask personal questions about how much money they make, how much money they have saved in the bank, the description of their most expensive jewelry or possessions. Exaggerations always work best in a role-play to bring out the point. But be sure to limit the types of personal questions.

In this role-play they may have appropriately maintained boundaries and politely changed the question. The most important lesson in this role-play is to refer back to the rules of the relationship, appropriate boundaries and unacceptable boundaries. The unacceptable response would be for the mentor to answer the questions in detail.

2. **Youth talks about crime.** In this case, playing the role of a youth, you begin to give details of a crime you were involved in either as a witness or a participant. Make it clear to the mentor that you were never arrested or adjudicated for this crime. You may even brag about how clever you were in the commission of this crime. If the mentor showed appropriate behavior, they would first advise the youth that if they continue with the discussion they would be obligated to give that information to appropriate authorities, such as a probation officer. The **inappropriate response** would be to continue to listen to the details and even be impressed. The object of this role-play is to set proper boundaries and advise youth that you would be obligated to pass on such information, but especially not have them be proud of past conduct.

3. **Youth attempts to get mentor to break rules.** In this role-play you may set it within the residential phase in a facility and attempt to manipulate the mentor into bringing you money or something else that has a cash value such as a roll of stamps. By exaggerating the role-play you may talk in a sincere tone and tell them that it is necessary to have the stamps to write to a sick grandmother. If you exaggerate the role-play, it can be humorous and diffuse any tension in the group. Most mentors will easily see that any attempt to get them to break rules is wrong and they can be firm but not harsh as they hold the limits and give the youth an understanding that they know the rules.

4. **Youth asks for large gift.** In this role-play set in the post-residential phase, it is approaching Christmas and the youth specifically asks for a gift with a high price tag, such as a $200 Play Station 2. Within the role-play they can appear needy or ask for the gift as a response to their showing up for meetings and

being good. When the role-play is successful, the mentor will tell them that gifts are not associated with expected behaviors and that gifts with a high price tag are not appropriate within the mentor/youth relationship. An unsuccessful role-play would be the mentor assuring them that they would give them large gifts they ask for.

5. **Mentor distracted.** In this role-play the trainer plays the mentor and the youth simply expresses a deep emotional feeling about any subject they choose. In this case, the trainer is playing a mentor who is sending poor body language in listening. As examples, there would be no eye contact, arms would be folded across the chest, and the mentor will periodically yawn or look at their watch. For the group, this is sometimes a humorous role-play but the feedback from the mentor playing the youth is often dramatic. The mentor is asked, "How did you feel?" And quite often they will say, "The person was not listening, looked bored or distracted, or I was not worthy of their time." This is a good role-play to bring awareness that is not simply words that convey listening but also facial expression and body language.

6. **Youth complains about parents.** In this role-play the trainer plays the youth and tries to engage the mentor in siding with them against a parent. This one has a very obvious teaching lesson. It is unsuccessful when the mentor empathizes with the youth and sides with them against a parent. Remember, if they agree with the youth's perspective it is better to keep it neutral and only empathize with how the youth feels but not take a side against a parent.

7. **Depression/suicide.** In this role-play the trainer plays a child and without being too overt sends out signals of being withdrawn, depressed or even hints at "leaving this world." A successful role-play is one in which the mentor advises the child they will have to inform other people because they are concerned about them. An unsuccessful role-play would be the mentor minimizing the signals or symptoms or even giving counseling type advice such as taking aspirin, getting more sleep, or simply praying about the issue. Based upon the material in the manual, depression and suicide are

too important a subject for a mentor to engage in superficial advice or even attempt psychological counseling.

8. **Breaking confidence.** In this role-play the trainer plays a teacher who attempts to get the mentor to give as much personal information about the youth, which has come from their relationship. Questions like "What do you talk about?" "What is the youth really thinking about me or school?" In a successful role-play, the mentor maintains confidentiality and says politely, "Those are confidential issues and the youth may choose to reveal them to you in your relationship. Maintaining confidence is the most important part of this role-play.

9. **Attempts to manipulate mentor.** In this role-play the teacher plays a police officer who is trying to get the mentor to turn the youth into a "snitch". In a manipulative but controlled manner, the police officer tries to get the mentor to obtain specific names and locations of peers in order to help them make an arrest. In a successful role-play, the mentor advises the police officer to talk with the probation officer or other members of the team. In an unsuccessful role-play, they will tell the police officers that they will cooperate fully and by doing so it jeopardizes their mentor/youth relationship and obviously violates trust.

10. **Youth tantrum.** In this role-play the trainer playing the youth engages in name-calling or even ridicules the mentor and has a child-like tantrum. In a successful role-play the mentor will not take the name-calling personally and will try to calm the youth or even terminate the meeting by telling them to consider the consequences of their behavior or uncontrolled anger. The trainer may consider a reversal of role and play the mentor and ask the mentor to have a temper tantrum. In this way they can exhibit the correct behavior and calm the youth.

11. **Being judgmental.** In this role-play the trainer may choose to exaggerate to make the point to ask the youth to speak about why they like MTV or rap music and then continually interrupt them

with a statement that starts with "But" and lectures or sermonizes on the evils of rap music or MTV and by doing so becomes judgmental. This is often a humorous role-play and the exaggerations are purposeful. A successful role-play will demonstrate that simply listening and asking why they like something helps to develop a relationship. Most adults can easily see why being judgmental can close down communication.

SUMMARY

Role-play is an effective way to demonstrate how difficult situations can be handled. It is easier for the mentor to remember the drama that they participated in and even the exaggeration of the situations, which can create humor, is a good teaching mechanism. Most adults will easily see the absurdity of certain extreme reactions, and even if they were inclined to engage in them, it will help them to think twice.

Within training the role-play helps assess the knowledge of the material in the training and is an effective training tool.

Be sure individuals playing the roles are volunteering. Try not to have one person play all the roles but have as many volunteers as possible. Sometimes a trainer will be surprised that someone who appears to be quiet can be rather effective within a role-play. You may have to help them to stay in the role, as your exaggerations will sometimes make other people laugh or stop the role-play. Tell them that they are acting and that their reactions do not represent what they would actually do as a mentor. This will help keep any laughter of the group from being interpreted as personal harassment toward the individual.

It is far better to have the trainer play the difficult or obstinate roles and have the mentor react as they normally would. Most mentors will make the right decisions and having read this book ahead of time will know how to maintain boundaries and rules. Even those who make mistakes in the role-play usually see the point intended.

Appendix

Appendix A

QUESTIONS MENTORS ASK ABOUT REPORTING ABUSE

Question 1: What if a youth has me promise not to tell anyone about abuse?

Answer: As the adult and the authority figure in a mentoring relationship, you must never make a promise that would betray your ability to keep a youth safe. You must simply tell them that there are some situations, like abuse, when you must refer to professionals who can protect the youth.

Question 2: Should I talk to a youth's parents or guardians?

Answer: There is no clear-cut answer here. If you believe the person committing the offense is a parent or guardian, they logically would not be the people to go to. If you think abuse is occurring from another authority figure in the community, then it would be wise to bring the parents into your confidence and decide upon a plan of action to help counsel the youth. Inform the program coordinator. Discretely confront the situation.

Question 3: Should I contact the Department of Juvenile Justice?

Answer: Yes, if the youth is either in residential phase of supervision or in the community, he or she remains under the jurisdiction of the Department of Juvenile Justice. There is a specific hotline for reporting the abuse of youth. It is 1-800-96-ABUSE (2-2873).

Question 4: Should I give details when calling the abuse hotline?

Answer: Yes, the more details you can provide, the more you will help authorities. Do not embarrass the youth, but do obtain a specific date and time and even the name of the person who committed the abuse. The rule is, the more details, the more it will help the overall situation, but be sensitive regarding sexual abuse. Allow the counselor or therapist to lead that discussion.

Question 5: What role should the mentor play?

Answer: Since you have established a relationship with the youth, you should be available to investigators should they require more information. You should also let the youth know that you care about them and want to protect them from any further abuse. Be supportive and affirming.

Question 6: How do you prepare the youth for the reporting of abuse?

Answer: The mentor should tell the youth that Child and Family Services, and possibly the police, may come to interview them. Assure the youth not to feel threatened and not to be fearful of any retaliation from the offending person.

Question 7: Can I report the abuse anonymously?

Answer: Yes, you can give as many details by phone and yet remain anonymous in reporting the abuse. Understand that all the reports taken by Child and Family Services are strictly confidential.

Question 8: What are the symptoms and types of sexual abuse?

Answer: The law defines what is sexual abuse for a minor.

Here are types of sexual abuse:

a) An adult should never touch a minor sexually or have the child touch them in any manner that is sexual.

b) A parent can talk about emerging sexuality with his or her own son or daughter, but an adult (including a mentor) should not be initiating sexual conversations with a minor.

c) At no time should an adult show a minor any pornographic literature or pornographic images in print or on the Internet.

d) An adult should never be exposing their private sexual parts to a minor, masturbate in front of them, or watch the child undressed via a hidden camera or a camera in a cell phone or any type of peephole.

e) A minor should never be stripped of their clothing for discipline or spanking by an adult not a parent.

f) Any form of photography of a minor for sexual purposes or involvement of a minor in pornography or prostitution is strictly forbidden by the law.

This is what sexual abuse does not include:

- A medical exam during which there is a third party in the examining room.
- The normal physical interaction between a parent and a child, which would include a kiss, a hug, or even a back rub. These are not, of course, activities the mentor should be engaged in.

APPLICATION TO MENTOR

The mentor relationship should remain above reproach. There is no need for anything beyond a pat on a shoulder for affirmation or a friendly handshake between the mentor and the youth. Use common sense. When in doubt, contact the program coordinator.

Remember there are many ways you can affirm a youth without misinterpretation. The first is through words like "You did a great job," "You really improved in this area," or "I like the way you express yourself." You can always show encouragement by a nod, a wink, a smile or a quick pat on the back. These are just as effective without sending any wrong signals.

Appendix B

MENTOR CONTACT INFORMATION

Name of youth	**Date of birth**
Youth's nickname	**Guardian's name**
Father's name	**Mother's name**
Parent's home phone	**Parent's cell phone**
Youth's mailing address	**Youth's cell phone**
Probation Officer	**Officer's phone**
Program Coordinator	**Coordinator's phone**
Chaplain	**Chaplain's phone**
Residential Phone Number	

Appendix C

Bibliography

Faith-Based Mentoring

Atkin, Ross, "The Mentor Touch; Youth groups recruit busy adults with better programs, fewer hours," **Christian Science Monitor,** Feb. 2, 2000.

Barnes, Tim & Mary Stiasny, Eds., **Mentoring: Marking it Work,** Bassett Press, Southampton, 1995.

Becker, J., **Mentoring High-Risk Kids,** Johnson Institute, Minneapolis, MN, 2004.

Benner, Dr. David, **Healing Emotional Wounds,** Baker Book House, Grand Rapids, MI, 1990.

Brendtro, Larry, **Reclaiming Youth At Risk: Our Hope for the Future,** National Educational Service, Bloomington, IN, 1990.

Davis, J., Relationships/Orange County: "One-on-One Adds Up for Mentors and At-Risk Youths," Orange County Edition, **Los Angeles Times,** May 3, 1995.

Decker, Cathleen, Wilson Urges Caring Adults to Mentor At-Risk Youths, **Los Angeles Times,** November 15, 1996.

Dobson, Dr. James, **Love Must Be Tough,** Word Publishing, Nashville, TN, 1996.

Dortch, Thomas and Joyner, Tom, **The Miracles of Mentoring: The Joy of Investing in Our Future,** Doubleday, 2000.

Freedman, M., **The Kindness of Strangers: Adult Mentors, Urban Youth, and the New Voluntarism,** Jossey Bass, San Francisco, 1993.

Furano, K. et al, **Big Brothers/Big Sisters: A Study of Program Practices,** Public/Private Ventures. Philadelphia, PA, 1993.

Larson, Scott, **At-Risk: Bringing Hope to Hurting Teens,** Group Publishing, Loveland, CO, June 1999.

McDowell, Josh, **Handbook on Counseling Youth,** Word Publishing, Dallas, TX, 1996.

McLean, Gordon, **Danger at Your Door,** Crossway Books, Westchester, IL, 1984.

McLean, Gordon, **Too Young to Die,** Tyndale House, Wheaton, IL, 1998.

Morrow, Kristine and Styles, Melanie, **Building Relationships With Youth in Program Settings: A Study of Big Brothers/Bit Sisters,** Public/Private Ventures, Philadelphia, 1995.

Mosqueda, P.F. and Paaich, R., **Mentoring Young People Makes a Difference,** Education Commission of the States, Denver, CO, 1990.

Parks, Sharon Daloz, **Big Questions, Worthy Dreams: Mentoring Young Adults in Their Search for Meaning, Purpose, and Faith,** Jossey-Bass, 2000.

Potts, Tom, "Volunteering at schools has many rewards," **The Dallas Morning News,** November 12, 2000.

Rhodes, Jean E, **Stand by Me: The Risks and Rewards of Mentoring Today's Youth** (The Family and Public Policy), Harvard University Press, March 2002.

Saito, R. N. and Blyth, D. A., **Understanding Mentoring Relationships,** Search Institute, Minneapolis, MN, 1992.

Seamands, **Healing of Memories,** Victor Books, Wheaton, IL, 1985.

Smalley, Gary, **The Blessing,** Thomas Nelson Publishers, Nashville, TN, 1976.

Smarto, Don, **Lost and Found: Ministry to Incarcerated Youth,** Frontline Press, Dallas, TX, 2004.

Smarto, Don, **Keeping Ex-Offenders Free,** Frontline Press, Dallas, TX, 2001.

Steele, Ralph, **Mentoring and the Rites of Passage for Youth.** Ravlon Books, 1998.

Taylor, A. S., & Bressler, J., **Mentoring Across Generations: Partnerships for Positive Youth Development,** Plenum, New York, 2000.

Veerman, David, **Reaching Out to Troubled Youth,** Victor Books, Wheaton, IL, 1987.

Appendix D

"Love is very patient and kind, never jealous or envious, never boastful or proud, never haughty or selfish or rude.

Love does not demand its own way.

It is not irritable or touchy.

It does not hold grudges or hardly even notice when others do it wrong.

It is never glad about injustice but rejoices whenever truth wins out.

If you love someone you will be loyal to him no matter what the cost."

I Corinthians 13:4-7

Appendix E

INTERVIEW WITH DWIGHT HARRIS

Dwight Harris is one of the most respected professionals in the juvenile justice system in America as the Executive Director of the Texas Youth Commission.

He oversees a residential population of 4,875 youth each year with an average length of stay of 20 months. His program has an average of 2,614 new commitments each year. Dwight Harris was named Executive Director of the Texas Youth Commission in 2004. As a career veteran, he has had 25 years of experience working his way up from a caseworker, a coordinator of a half-way house, an assistant superintendent of a state school to the Deputy Director's position.

Mr. Harris has an Associate's Degree in Psychology, a Bachelor's Degree in Sociology, and Master's in Business and Administration, and additionally studied at the University of California Law School.

A capable administrator, Mr. Harris is responsible for an annual budget of 251.6 million dollars, a work force of 4,700 employees and nearly 8,000 juvenile offenders, both in residential placement and parole supervision.

The author interviewed Mr. Harris in his Austin, Texas, office in July 2006.

DS (Don Smarto): What is your vision for the future as Executive Director of the Texas Youth Commission?

DH (Mr. Harris): Well, Don, I am really past the age of retirement because of my years with the Texas Youth Commission and that is a good thing. I do not have to worry about a political agenda. I am here because I want to help as many youth as I can.

DS: If you had more money, what would your first priority be?

DH: It would certainly not be more buildings. I think we should have smaller facilities and smaller populations so we can put an emphasis on relationships. Currently we are understaffed and some people have to work 10 to 12 hour shifts and others on weekends without overtime. These are dedicated people, but they need to be compensated properly. So, I would first put the money into hiring more staff, then creating smaller facilities with smaller youth populations.

DS: Do you think it is harder to be a young person in today's society?

DH: In many ways I do. You know, they know more and they have seen more. In fact I recently discovered that over half of the youth in our facilities have seen someone murdered! Now, you and I know that is not right. Children should not have to view such things, not to mention know of them. We've always had problems with drugs and lack of education, but I believe there is more permissiveness and even evil in today's world.

DS: What role does poverty play?

DH: I grew up in a farm community. You might say we were poor, but education was always an important value. I was very fortunate to have a strong family, but there are many young people today who are into the third and fourth generation of poverty. Without question, poverty is one of the causes of crime.

DS: Do you think the welfare system has helped?

DH: I actually think the welfare system has hurt us. Even though there were good intentions, it has sent a message to a woman that she can have a baby and get a paycheck without having a man in her life. It has created dependency. It has contributed to this massive problem of missing fathers. Welfare has also hurt people's self-esteem and their pride.

DS: Where do you think government's dollar should be <u>best</u> spent?

DH: I think most professionals would agree "early intervention". It's not too late when we're working with these young people, but our median age is 16, and we are already seeing problems when they are seven and eight. We need more community programs, especially after-school programs, and we need more involvement from the church and volunteers.

DS: Some say that movies and television are making youth more violent. Do you agree?

DH: Well, my answer is yes and no. The box (television) dictates values. Marshall McLuhan said that "the medium **is** the message". I don't believe it's the cause of violence, but for those who are already predisposed, it pushes them over the edge. It is disturbing for the borderline youth. The values of leading characters in TV shows have degenerated. And seeing graphic violence desensitizes a young person. I am personally offended by the rap music with lyrics that disrespect mothers, daughters and sisters. It is not the complete cause, but the movies, television and rap music do not contribute to a young person's healthy thinking.

DS: How do gangs factor in?

DH: Gangs are clearly a substitute for a family that is usually not there. Again, missing fathers contribute to the allure that gangs have for young people. The gangs offer them employment, even though negative such as dealing drugs, and food, clothes and a sense of belonging, which, after all, is what family is all about.

DS: With only three percent of juveniles referred to the court system ending up in the Texas Youth Commission, do you think incarceration is destructive?

DH: Unfortunately, there are some very violent offenders, although a small percentage, who do need to be locked up for the protection of the community, but sadly I have to say that some youth have it better in a facility. The fact that they have three meals a day, clean clothes, discipline, proper bedding, caring people and education is a statement that points back to the neglect of these young people. They are often the victims of poor parenting or missing parents.

DS: When you were younger, did you have a mentor?

DH: Yes, I had many mentors. I was mentored by teachers, coaches, uncles and my father. And those people had a very important influence on my life. They gave me the values of being a good citizen, a hard worker, a respect for law and a desire for education. Most of us would not be in positions of leadership without the mentors in our lives.

DS: What are other values of mentoring?

DH: Clearly youth need role models. They are going to find them one way or another. They may be drug dealers and gang leaders. They may be rap artists with negative lyrics. Poor role models lead them down the wrong path, but we are fortunate at TYC (Texas Youth Commission) to have many volunteers, often from churches, who are involved in mentoring and really making a difference in young people's lives

DS: What would change if there were no mentors?

DH: Well, I am a firm believer that we need the spiritual element. We are involved in re-socialization, in cognitive treatment which affects how they think, but we also need volunteers who can provide support, encouragement, and who are actually a great help to our staff. I wish we had one mentor for every youth in our system.

DS: You mentioned re-socialization; can you explain that?

DH: Re-socialization is one of our treatment plans. We obviously want these children to have lasting change and become better people. Otherwise they are just "doing time" and that is always wasted time. In group counseling we try to determine why they make bad choices. We demonstrate that in order to have change, they need a plan, and that plan includes education, work, re-integration to the family as well as personal changes.

263

DS: Professionals talk of sociopaths that have no conscience. What is your opinion?

DH: Well, clearly there are some youth that can hurt people and do not feel bad. Fortunately they are a very small percentage, less than a half of one percent. We work with them hoping to bring them toward empathy and helping them to realize that their crimes just don't hurt victims but also their family, the victim's family, the community and themselves. I believe it is as simple as the Golden Rule. We try to help these young people understand that positive values and respect for people's rights are more acceptable than criminal values.

DS: Please go back to cognitive behavior?

DH: We know that how people think affects how they behave. So we try to point out, usually in group, their thinking errors. This takes time, of course. Eventually, you will discover an offense cycle in a young person's life. In order to break that cycle, they have to think in new ways and new directions. If you will, they have to replace the old values with new values.

DS: Is this successful?

DH: Yes, in many cases it is successful. As I said, it takes time, but often through education and talking about behavioral rules, we can help them to avoid the poor thinking of the past.

DS: If we can help young people to learn how to solve their problems, to manage their anger, and to develop better communication skills, are there other areas needed?

DH: Don, I'm aware of the **Parenting Seminar** you do for boys at TYC who have fathered children. That's an example of a contribution that really helps us. It fits exactly into the kind of programming that we do.

DS: What gives you reason for hope?

DH: Well, I personally believe in God and I believe that none of these youth are born a delinquent. They are not born a criminal. Many of them feel unwanted and unworthy. We can supply good food, clean clothes, opportunities for exercise and education, but there clearly has to be a spiritual dimension. I believe in the power of God in changing people. A ministry like yours, **Youth Direct**, is making a great difference. The volunteers supply needs that our staff simply cannot, like Bible studies and mentoring. As long as I am at this helm, there will always be a place for the spiritual.

DS: Is there any last thing you would like to say?

DH: If we look at the zip codes, we can tell very quickly where these youth are coming from. We know that poverty is a great influence. And missing fathers have created a great part of the problem we witness. But I am a positive person who believes we are really making progress. I am excited by the number of volunteers and ministries that come into our facilities and care about these young people as our staff does. I really believe mentoring is essential to help these young people grow. They need adults, men and women, who they can look up to and can teach them lessons. We all learn from the mistakes we have made in life.

DS: Mr. Harris, thank you for your time.

DH: You are more than welcome, Don. I hope your ministry and your volunteers continue to work with the Texas Youth Commission for many years to come.